UNLOCKING LOVE

10 Keys to Finding the Love of Your Life

(Even If It's You)

James Michael Sama

Introduction

—

I was always taught to properly greet someone at the beginning of an interaction, and since that's precisely what this is, I'd like to extend a warm welcome to you for being part of this journey with myself, and millions of others.

You see, we are navigating a terrain in human history for the very first time. Technology, social media, shifting gender roles (or elimination of them), relationship norms — you name it, it's changing.

So, it's natural that we are confused. It's natural to take a little extra time struggling to find our place in the world, whether it be professionally, or personally. In this book, I'd like to have a discussion with you about the best way(s) to go about it, and how we can all live happier, healthier lives with more fulfilling relationships.

Believe me, I don't claim to be an expert on topics of life and love. I have, though, spent the past 5 years writing articles that have been read over 50 million times and translated into multiple different languages. I have spoken to audiences from 50 to 50,000 people across the United States. I have had literally thousands of conversations with individuals about their frustrations — and triumphs — in their relationships and personal lives.

Growing up, I always observed my parents and grandparents in their relationships. They were "old school" romantic, a bit cheesy at times. Traditional, but also modern (my parents anyway...my grandparents, not so much). I watched my mother be at home with my brother and me all the time, but she did it while she was running her own business, which she still successfully owns and operates more than 30 years later. My dad, even more romantic and cheesy than I am (sorry, dad), still acts this way towards my mom.

This is what I saw as *normal* growing up. I thought that the way to a woman's heart was through romantic gestures and being *just a little bit* over the top. Ah, the reality check awaiting me in my teenage years...a rude awakening. On top of that, I never had much confidence growing up. I was a bit shy, a bit overweight, a bit socially awkward.

So, naturally, eventually I got tired of going to dances alone and being rejected for dates. I decided to educate myself on human dynamics and the way we all interact in different areas of life. I reinvented myself — repeatedly. I shredded the pounds away — well, most of them. And, most of all, I began to notice a disconnect between what I thought would make people happy, and what people were actually doing when it came to dating and relationships. This is why I began to write my blog, to express my opinions on what I had seen work in marriages and relationships in the past.

The lessons I've learned, the experiences I've had, the people I've met, the failures I've faced, and the successes I've enjoyed, have helped me to compile what I feel are ten keys we all need to unlock the doors on our journey to finding happiness. Whether you are in a relationship, or spreading your wings and flying solo, this process will help you find your path in your own unique way.

We are all works in progress, on our own paths of discovery and self-creation. I do not write this to place myself above you or to teach you lessons which I do not practice in my daily life, myself. I am here to walk beside you as a brother on this journey, learning and growing, as you are. To learn from you, as I learn from every person and experience that life brings me.

I have walked a variety of paths in my life. I have been a martial arts instructor, a salesman, a street racer, an athlete, a lover, a fighter, a friend. I have been happy, and I have been to the depths of whiskey bottles after breakups. I have run the gamut and — hopefully — have come out stronger on the other side.

Most recently, I decided to take my own advice and be true to myself. I packed a single suitcase, sold all of my furniture, moved out of my apartment, left my car for sale, and moved 3,000 miles from Boston to Hollywood. I did this because I had faced enough failure and dead ends to understand the road I shouldn't be on, and to envision the one I needed to be on. I have absorbed pieces of every experience and relationship that have molded me into the person that I am today, and continue to, during every waking second.

[Disclaimer] I do not claim to be an expert, a guru, a master, or one bestowed with infinite wisdom. I do not have formal training or a professional license. I am not a therapist, or a psychiatrist. I couldn't even tell you the difference between the two. I do not intend for this book to be a replacement for professional opinion, nor do I intend it to be the sole source of your life's decision-making. As are the 700+ articles I have written up to this point, this book is a projection of my personal opinions, as formed by the years I have lived thus far and the experiences that have filled them. I have observed, learned, self-educated, faltered, stumbled, fallen, and failed (repeatedly).

I have been burned in relationships, heartbroken, and walked away from by women I thought I was going to spend my life with. I do not come to you wearing rose-colored glasses. I do not come to you with a book telling you that everything is going to be okay, or easy, or positive all the time. I come to you with real life experiences and the lessons from them seared into my heart and mind. I come to you with realism, seasoned with optimism and hope.

You may not like everything you read in this book, but it's not my responsibility to feed you from a sugar-coated spoon. It's my responsibility to bring you through a journey of self-discovery that will hopefully inspire you, give you hope, and bring you some clarity in a world full of noise and static.

I invite you to a journey I have taken myself, and continue to take each and every day. There is no finish line, there is no final destination. Life is constantly morphing and evolving around us, and we have to adapt and adjust as seamlessly as possible. The one thing that remains constant in this world is the person you are. You are the center of your universe, you are the main character in your own story. You are the person who gets to decide how to live this life and who you want to bring along the journey with you.

I am honored that you have chosen to take me along on your journey, as I take you along on mine. I am not here to walk in front of you, I am here to walk alongside you as a teammate.

Every journey begins with a single step, every house begins with a foundation, and, *every book begins with a first chapter.*

CHAPTER ONE

Recognizing Your Own Self Worth

—

I have learned that there is one single foundational reality that needs to be established before you can begin any journey. That foundational reality is the confidence in yourself to understand that you are able to, and deserve to, actually reach the destination.

Growing up, I spent the majority of my life more than a little chubby. You know, those damn Italian households where there's as much food around as there is oxygen. That, combined with a lack of self-control, kept me shopping in the XL section through most of high school.

I'm not saying you need to look a certain way in order to be confident in yourself, but we all feel these things in different ways. For me, I was always self-conscious about the way I looked, so I would never put myself out there much. I was bullied, ridiculed, jumped in the locker room, and developed a consistent habit of getting rejected for dates.

Needless to say, I didn't quite have the "strut" down just yet. And because of this, my level of confidence perpetually lived in the shitter while I watched everyone around me go to parties, date the pretty girls, and score all the touchdowns.

It wasn't until I got into college that I really began to shed the weight and develop confidence in myself. Some could argue, a bit too much confidence, but sometimes we need to play around on the spectrum before we find our comfortable spots. I completely changed the way I looked (repeatedly), and had quite the MySpace page, if I do say so myself.

For those of you reading this who have no idea what MySpace is, just think Facebook with flashing graphics and music and obnoxious photos that would get you fired from your jobs immediately.

The thing that MySpace allowed me to do, though, was project myself to the world in the way that I felt was an accurate depiction of who I was. I could choose the colors, music, photos, and overall *brand* that I wanted people to see. In doing so, I started to get positive feedback from people I'd never met, friend requests, messages, and even began to frequently meet women in real life, off of the site.

Naturally, I started to question, *was I really ugly*? Or had I been conditioned by my social circles to see myself in a different light rather than being able to see what was actual reality.

And, thanks to Tom (another MySpace reference), my entire path of life shifted in that instant. I started observing other people. What images were getting the most feedback? Whose style did I like the most that I could learn from? What kind of places were these "cool people" hanging around, places I had never seen before?

I stopped being a victim of circumstance and decided to start creating the life I wanted to live. I understood that it was possible, because I was seeing other people doing it. I was being invited places, and was actually experiencing being in these environments. I finally understood that the life I wanted to live wasn't something I'd only be able to watch other people partaking in, I could *actually live it.*

A funny thing happens when you realize that you can live the life you've always wanted to live. You start to actually do it.

You start putting yourself into situations where you meet higher quality people. You start to apply for the jobs you didn't think you'd have a chance at getting. You start to build momentum in the direction you want to go in. Progress breeds consistency, because you're seeing results.

Small victories. Baby steps. More time in the gym. An interview for the job you wanted, but not quite getting it (yet). A smile and a conversation with the pretty girl at the bar, but not quite getting her number (yet). An investor telling you that your business is a great idea, but not being handed a check for it (yet).

Things start happening for you, simply because you continue to learn, grow, and improve. You learn from your mistakes, but you do not let them stop you, because you know that they can't. The only thing that can stop you is the decision to quit. Not a decision that you're going to make.

TRANSLATING LIFE TO LOVE

Then, it hits you. If you are this strong, confident, ambitious, driven individual with so much to offer to the world, then why don't you deserve to be with a person who recognizes these qualities in you, and appreciates you for them? Someone who loves and cares for you, as you would for him or her? Someone who has also put in the work to become the person who can thrive either individually, or alongside a teammate in a relationship?

The clarity feels like a bracingly cold wave washing over you in the ocean on a summer day: *You do deserve it.*

You deserve the same love that you've been watching the people around you find all of these years. You deserve to receive the same love that you've been aching to give to another human being. You have worked, and fought, and struggled to become the person you are proud to be — the person someone should be proud to *be with* as well.

Here's the thing, though. You may have noticed that the struggle you've gone through up to this point — at least, the one I'm illustrating — has absolutely nothing to do with actually *being in a relationship*. It has nothing to do with how to act on a first date, or how many hours you should wait to text someone back, or where the best places are to meet men or women. *That's because you need to figure your own shit out first.*

A lot of people ask me where they can meet quality men or women. They ask me what to say, what to do, how to act, what to wear. How to *attract* other people — keeping the focus on the *how* and not the *why*.

Why — as in, why should this person be attracted to you?

Why are you deserving of a happy relationship?

Why are you ready to give yourself to someone, fully?

Why is someone going to be drawn to you over everyone else?

Did these questions sting a little bit? Perhaps that's why nobody asks them. Perhaps that's why *you* haven't asked them of yourself. And, perhaps, that's why so many people have a hard time actually finding someone they are happy with, because they haven't fully developed *themselves* as a desirable partner.

What are the best things you can do in order to attract the type of person you want to be with?

Be attractive.

That's right, be attractive. There's your big secret. You could probably put this book down right now and know all that you need to (please don't...) but the question is, what does it mean to *be attractive?*

I am certainly not suggesting that you need to look a certain way, dress a certain way, or have any specific type of appearance in order to be desirable to the man or woman of your dreams. What I am suggesting, is that you live your life in a way that draws people to it. You live your life with passion, voracity, energy, *purpose.*

Live your life on purpose, by purpose, and with purpose.

Do not continue allowing life to simply happen around you. Do not continue passively accepting what your hours, days, weeks, months, or *years* drop in your lap and allowing it to be called a *life*. A life is something you create for yourself. It is something you decide on, and take action on. It is something that you have to consciously take control of every single day. If you don't, it's going to rule you. It's going to stifle your progress. It's going to rob you of your happiness, like a thief in the night, who while you are sleeping takes everything you value.

Is this the way you want to live your life?

I refuse. I refuse to live my life in this way, and I refuse to sit by while you live your life this way. I refuse to accept the concept that you are happy and content without making your own choices for what you want your life to look like. I reject the reality that you are doing the absolute best you can at every moment of the day. I refuse to accept that you cannot do better than you are doing at this very second.

You must *choose* love. You must *choose* happiness. You must *choose* your path — and then *walk it with intention.* That is why you are reading this book, and that is why I wrote this book. I made the self-discovery a long time ago that I wasn't going to live life on anyone else's terms — and you know what? It can absolutely suck.

It sucks to create your own path. It sucks to feel like you're the only person who thinks the way you do. It sucks to wonder if you're ever going to be able to create stability for yourself. It sucks to wonder if anyone is actually going to *love you for you.* It sucks to be sitting alone on the weekend staring at the "*0 notifications*" message on your phone, taunting you.

It sucks, but you know what? Anything that's worthwhile is going to suck at first. Anything that's going to allow you to create the life you want to live, is going to be riddled with roadblocks and speed bumps. It's going to suck *because it's worth it, and nothing worthwhile comes easily.* It's going to suck because you may feel alone as you break free from your tribe in order to find one that better suits you.

Most people will look at this journey and psych themselves out. They'll become overwhelmed, or scared, or nervous, or they'll look at the *total distance* they need to go between where they currently are and where they want to be. The truth is, it is many small steps, many measurable short-term goals, that eventually accumulate to create one continuous path, along which, there are a plethora of enjoyable experiences.

But, you must step outside of your comfort zone and take the first step — for that is where the magic awaits you.

PUTTING YOUR CHRISTMAS TREE IN THE STAND

As I've mentioned, my background is Italian. A lot of our family traditions revolve around holidays, and with no disrespect to anyone else's religion, I'm going to draw on my background to illustrate an idea. Whether you usually have a Christmas tree or a solstice tree, or are going to have to imagine that, consider for a moment the complicated task of decorating it.

What about putting the ornaments on the tree *before* you get it secured in the stand? Sounds a bit ridiculous, doesn't it? This is because even the prettiest things can come crashing down if they don't have the proper foundation to stand on. The same goes for you and your relationships with other people.

Much like putting the tree in the stand, this is the hardest part of the process. Developing your self-worth is hard work. It takes time, effort, energy, criticism, failures, feedback from others, falling on your ass, and — standing up again. And again. And again.

Most people think that confidence is something that comes naturally. Either you have it, or you don't. No, screw that. Confidence is something you choose, it's something you build, it's something you cultivate over time. And, it is hard friggin' work. It is not glamorous, or pretty. Your self-worth is the messy, shitty part of putting up that Christmas tree when the dirt and sticky resin from the stump are on your hands and the needles have rained over your head to the point where you don't know where your hair ends and the tree begins.

It's the heavy lifting, the hoisting of that sucker up to the ceiling. The concern that one of your vertebrae is going to fling itself across the room like a discus at the Olympics. It can hurt, it can suck, and you know what? Sometimes you're going to need to call a friend to help you. You can't always do it by yourself.

The people you call to help you put up the tree are the people you can truly count on in your life. Most people are going to visit your house when the tree is up, and see all of the pretty lights and decorations. They will enjoy the final product and you can stand there and be proud of your work, but you know what? Those people had no idea what you looked like covered in dirt and needles.

Those people weren't there when the water spilled all over the floor and you had to clean it up. They weren't there when you were just about to drag the stupid thing outside and light it on fire. They weren't there when you were just about ready to give up.

But, you know what? They love and appreciate the final product. The person you have worked so hard to become. They don't see you sweating in the gym or crunching numbers for your business at all hours. They won't be there during your 7-mile runs while you're feeding your brain with inspirational podcasts and audiobooks. They won't be sitting next to you when you're taking your online classes to further advance yourself in life.

Chapter One

And sometimes, the people who start the journey with you, do not end it with you. Sometimes they don't support you the way you'd hoped, or acknowledge your efforts, or even understand why you're doing what you're doing. Some people simply want to hitch themselves to your wagon and revel in your success — but those are not the people for you.

I often hear stories about couples who are financially successful. Sometimes, assumptions are made about the reasons why they are together, or in a more stereotypical sense, they wonder if the woman is just with the man for his money. People wonder this same way they wonder if the man is just with the woman for her looks. It is an unfortunate reality of our society that may never be broken, but, on to the point...

The thing I find fascinating and inspiring about some of these stories, is when you hear the couple tell of the times that they were raising three children in a two-bedroom house with one bathroom. Perhaps they emigrated from a country where food was lacking, where they needed to stand in line for rations of milk. I once dated a woman from Moscow who had this exact story. Her father is now more than a little successful.

Perhaps they have a story of escaping conflict, or being nearly homeless, or being *actually* homeless. Maybe they needed to find cousins or friends to babysit because they both needed to work multiple jobs just to pay the bills and couldn't afford a babysitter. These are the relationships that last — do you know why?

Because they are built on a foundation of commitment. They are built upon the understanding that facing hard times together does not mean you give up on the very core of your existence — the relationship with the person who is by your side during all of the hardships. I am not talking about arguments between partners. I am not talking about butting heads or clashing egos. I am not talking about struggles *in the relationship*. I am talking about struggles that come our way in our everyday lives *while we are in a relationship*.

These are the couples who last because they were together when the man didn't even have a car, and the wife couldn't afford makeup. We make judgments based on what we see in the present day — we do this with everyone — when in reality we are simply catching a single frame of their life's movie.

Chapter One

None of us know what brought an individual or a couple to the place they are in now, and how strong their bond has become through facing challenges that we may never learn about.

The struggles you face in private give you the strength you project in public. And, more than that, they gives you the self-worth and confidence to understand that you damn well deserve what you've worked so hard for: Happiness.

CHAPTER TWO

Defining Your Happiness

—

Now that you've internalized the reality that you do, in fact, deserve happiness — what the hell does that even mean? Most people go throughout their days understanding that they can do better than they're doing, but then, why don't they actually do it?

When I used to have a daily commute (UGH, right?), I would make a habit of trying to smile at other drivers who were stuck in the same miserable traffic as I was. Do you know what I noticed the most? Not only was everyone accutely miserable, they were so focused on the brake lights on the car in front of them, that I couldn't even get their eye contact.

First of all, people, *be aware of your surroundings! This is dangerous!* Nobody seems to pay attention to what the hell is happening around them. Want to switch lanes? Sure, let's just mindlessly drift to the next lane and hope the person we're about to smash into is actually paying attention. Ah, but I digress.

The point here is that it takes more than just *knowing* you *deserve* happiness in order to find it. It takes real, clear *action* to move towards it.

One thing you'll learn about me quickly (if you haven't already) is that I like speaking in analogies. I mean, I just talked about your self-worth as if it were equal to putting up a Christmas tree —where the hell did that come from?

This time around, let's continue on the same road with comparison to driving. See what I did there?

You've gotten in your car to go to Happytown, time to put the address in the navigation.

Shit.

Where are you even going? I guess you can figure it out on the way. Life is a journey, after all. This is how I lived my life for a long time. I was enjoying the open road and figuring that I'd stumble upon happiness when I saw the exit coming up. It's gotta be up here somewhere. I just saw someone nearby who had it, I'm sure they were coming back from wherever I'm headed. That has to mean I'm going in the right direction.

Does this sound familiar? I'm betting either you've driven down the same road, or know someone who has. Maybe you're doing it right now.

STOP. HIT THE BRAKES. SCREECH TO A HALT.

In life and in love, happiness is not simply something we stumble upon or find when we reach a certain destination. Happiness is not a set of circumstances. It is not an accomplishment, *it is not a relationship.*

While you're driving around in a million different directions trying to "find" happiness, the reality is that it has been sitting right in the car next to you the whole time. It's something that comes from within you, something you decide to create yourself. Something you have access to at this very moment. If you're not happy right now — *why the hell not?* I know, I know, it's because you're waiting for your next paycheck to come in and you can't do something fun with your friends tonight. It's because your Mr. or Ms. Right hasn't made their way to you yet. *It's because the fucking wifi is down!*

Whatever the reason is that you're telling yourself you're not happy — listen to me — it's bullshit. It's absolute bullshit that you cannot be happy until you find a certain set of circumstances, do you know why? Because if that's how you approach the concept of happiness, it is always going to be dependent on something that you cannot control. You will always be a slave to happiness rather than its master. You will always be looking, searching, yearning for something that you will never find in the places where you're looking.

I think this is a big problem in our society today, because we are constantly bombarded with advertisements and images of things that are supposed to bring us happiness. The faster car, the more advanced phone, the nicer house, *the better looking significant other — am I right?*

Ah, there's the rub! We are always looking for the next best thing, and simultaneously wondering why the hell nobody is happy. That's not how happiness works! We cannot keep looking outside of ourselves for something that can only come from within. Do you know what happens if we do that?

They keep moving the exit sign!

I thought it was right up here, this is what the navigation says. Did they move it? *They must have moved it.* Johnny told me it was right here. I guess I'll have to keep driving until I find it.

It is not hard to see the root of the problem with this way of thinking. If we place our happiness on an external source, we always risk losing it. It could disappear, or be taken away, or simply not ever be found in the first place. And if we don't take the time to actually cultivate it within ourselves, we will never actually carry it with us. Do you see where I'm going with this? *It has to be inside of you, first, before you can project happiness into your everyday life.*

You can't go to a party and expect to find the gift you're bringing on the doorstep. You've got to have it with you first, in order to bring it with you. Hey, look, another analogy.

But, it's not that easy, James! I can't just wake up one day and decide to be happy, life is too hard. Yeah, no shit. That's the point. You can't just wake up and decide to be happy, you've got to put in the time, the effort, the sweat, and the tears, to figure out what that means to you. You've got to fail (again), you've got to hit roadblocks (are you sick of my analogies yet?), you've got to figure this stuff out for you, as an individual.

Nobody can tell you what it means for you to be happy. Nobody can fit you into a mold that you haven't created for yourself. Nobody can give this to you as a gift. You've got to figure it out on your own, and it takes work.

Think about what a future relationship may look like for you. Don't think about what your parents want for you. Don't think about the guilt trip your grandmother is going to give you over the holidays this year. Don't think about the path your friends have taken. *This is about you. And sometimes, what you want is not actually what you need.*

I can't tell you how many young men and women I have talked to whose stories sound something like this:

When my parents were my age, they were already married with 3 kids and had a house, a pension, a 401k, a retirement plan, a timeshare, a giant Cadillac, and a friggin' picket fence. Here I am wondering how many cat videos I can watch during my 15-minute break at work.

Well, times have changed. Expenses have changed, the job market has changed, and societal expectations and realities have *absolutely changed.* We do not live by the same rules or under the same roof (literally and figuratively) as generations past, and therefore we cannot judge ourselves using the same set of benchmarks. If you are reading this and you are of the age where you've experienced these societal changes firsthand, you know exactly what I am talking about.

Each of us looks to the generation before us for wisdom and guidance, but we also look to them for the ways in which we could improve our generation to allow a better foundation for the ones that come after us. We all want to leave a better world for our children, right? We all want our children to live a better life than we did, right? Yes, great, we agree — but *looking out for their well-being does not mean you have to sacrifice your own.*

You can learn from past generations and take hints from them. Perhaps you admire the relationship of a couple who's close to you — how do they communicate with each other? How do they interact? How do they handle conflict? Do you wonder how they always seem to be getting along, and extinguishing their disagreements before the flames take hold and a small misunderstanding explodes into a full-blown argument? Good! Interview them! Ask them questions! See what makes them tick and find out what the foundation of their relationship looks like.

You need to define and establish what this happiness looks like for you, and you've got to do it *while you're single*. This needs to be of highest priority while you're single because you need to make sure you're getting into the right relationship with the right person when he or she comes along. If you haven't taken the time to define what this looks like for you, how are you going to know when you find it?

Think about how you live your life when you're single. Do you go out every night? Would you rather binge-watch your favorite TV show all weekend? Do you want family? Do you think kids are the spawn of Satan? Do you work a traditional 9 –5, or does that sound like the ultimate form of torture? Envision the type of future you want for yourself, aligned with how you're happiest spending your time when you're single.

These seemingly benign, commonsense questions, are some of the most important that you can honestly answer for yourself, because they literally lay the framework for how you are going to live your life. They help you to define your values and your beliefs about what type of future you are moving towards, and therefore what kind of partner would be best suited for your life.

I'm not one of those people who subscribes to the idea of having a checklist of traits and attributes of the ideal partner I'm looking for, but I absolutely think having a *conceptual* vision of who they are is very important. Physical attraction is a given — that is an absolute necessity when maintaining a long -term relationship — but it is simply not enough to hold two people together through the waves that you must ride on the ocean of life. Or, the speedbumps on the road, if you will.

A lot of this conceptual vision is going to come from your relationships that haven't worked out. They're going to help teach you what you do and don't want in and from a partner. The key is to actually see these experiences as opportunities to learn, rather than letting them drag you down. Breakups are depressing, no doubt, but they also help you as you're becoming the person you're actually meant to be in the long run. If a relationship doesn't bring you what you want, then you can walk away from it with a learning experience that has helped teach you what you *don't* want.

Additionally, you can also learn the positives from past relationships. I know so many people who write off all of their exes and talk about what a terrible person they were. This has always fascinated me--the idea of condemning to hell a person with whom you shared life experiences with, shared your body with, your family with, holidays with — *there must have been something good about them, or you're just making the same, really shitty choices, repeatedly, and not learning anything.*

So, be open to what you can learn from your failed relationships, as well, even the negative experiences. Be mature enough to acknowledge the parts of your exes and past relationships that brought you happiness at the time. These are the lessons that are going to help you define what you *do* want in a partner and from a relationship.

NOW, AT LEAST, YOU CAN SET AN ADDRESS IN YOUR NAVIGATION.

FEELING BETTER ALREADY, EH?

CHAPTER THREE
Sources of Sadness

—

As important as it is to define what makes you happy in life and in love, it is equally (or perhaps even more so) important to define what doesn't. *Shit, man, this is getting complicated.*

Now, perhaps, it's easier to see why so many people settle

into relationships that don't truly bring them fulfillment. Most people don't take the time to truly establish their own self-worth (and therefore, boundaries and standards), and even fewer people take the time to define what they *truly* want and *need* in a relationship. Fewer still, will put in the work to define what they *don't* want.

I honestly believe this is not only a product of the societal pressure to be coupled, but also the human nature of yearning to be loved and accepted. As we continue to become more of an online-centric society, we are slowly losing our grip on genuine human connection and face-to-face interaction. Ironic, isn't it-- that we can be *so connected to everyone all the time,* but somehow feel more disconnected than ever? This leads to so many of us setting a much lower bar as to what we expect from others, I believe, because we are so desperately yearning for, and therefore accepting, whatever we can get from people.

Just because someone has some of the good qualities you're looking for doesn't mean you should overlook negative qualities. (Disclaimer: I'm not telling you to run away screaming the second a single red flag goes up. Relationships are about understanding and compromising — nobody is perfect).

Think about the small things that irked you in the beginning of your previous relationships, but morphed into something apocalyptic after being together for a year. Think about the time that, with stars in your eyes, you overlooked someone's desire to live in the country, when you had zero desire to leave the city. *It's not really a big deal, we'll figure it out. We'll cross that bridge when we come to it. Holy shit, the bridge is on fire!*

Seemingly benign things may be overlookable (I'm kind of surprised that's actually a word) at the time, but when you actually need to address the reality of the situation, these "tiny" little things can literally pull you apart. This is why looking into the future is important. Maybe if you're reading this at a young age, it's not that much of a concern for you yet, but for those of us who have already gone through the phases of flings and one-night-stands and summer romances, we're more equipped to understand the importance of long-term compatibility. Otherwise, what's the point of even dating someone in the first place?

Learning from other people's experiences, and being honest with yourself about your own, is a valuable practice in this area of a relationship. *Believe me — I know it's easy to have judgment clouded by feelings.* Oh, they're not really like that, though. But Bobby was different! Susan was horrible! MY boyfriend/girlfriend is a good person... deep down.

Stop making excuses for abhorrent behavior. We need a healthy balance of logic and emotion when entering a relationship, and this is where a lot of people get tripped up and tangled. Things start out hot and heavy, everything is wonderful, and the small little things that bug you get overlooked. You may tell your friend, who will express concern, but screw that. They don't know this person like you do. They may have faced a similar challenge in a past relationship that ended in disaster, but that's not going to happen to you. This person is different, despite the mounting number of red flags.

I seemed to have misplaced the "sarcasm" font, but perhaps you're picking up on my tone, here. Sorry, it's the Bostonian in me.

I'm being real with you here because I understand the feeling. I understand what it's like to enjoy someone's company *when things are good* and use that as a justification for when things are bad. Please remember my disclaimer that I'm not telling you that everything needs to be perfect (it never is) and you should bounce at the first sight of something that raises eyebrows. Just the opposite, actually. I'm encouraging you to understand what is truly a deal breaker for you, and what isn't. What are you willing to compromise on, and what is going to drive you absolutely bonkers in the long run, becoming unforgiveable?

Where is the balance between someone being chill, and someone being apathetic? Are you *Super Type-A* and they are *Super Type-B?* Are you a Gemini and they're a Virgo? (RUN). Just kidding. Sort of.

Sometimes we just have natural tendencies that don't line up with those of other people. It doesn't make either party better or worse than the other — *it's about compatibility.* Your own deal breakers don't have to be as serious and obvious as mistreatment, cheating, abuse (SERIOUSLY, RUN), or a

general lack of effort. Deal breakers can simply be puzzle pieces whose edges don't quite align, *but definitely need to be taken
seriously.*

Particularly as we get older, I see *so many* people who stay
in situations just because they don't want to start at the beginning. *Ugh, I can't break up with them because then I'm going to
have to meet someone new and start all over.* Well, damn right
you are! And hopefully it'll be with someone who actually puts
in an effort and matches up with your personality and wants
the same future as you — because you've taken the time to
learn from the experiences of your past!

But, alas, most people simply continue on the path they've
forged because they figure they've already invested the amount
of time that brought them here, so they might as well keep
going. *Hey man, you're on the wrong road! Continuing in this
direction ain't gonna bring you to the right one! U-turn! U-turn!*

You have to be willing recalculate when you discover
you're going the wrong direction, no matter how far you've
gone. Stop refueling the car to continue on the wrong path.

Stop ignoring bad behavior. If you have a puppy who tears up your furniture every time you leave the house, but you give him a treat when you get home, *why would he stop tearing up the furniture?*

Be honest with yourself — remember that strength isn't just about holding on, sometimes it's about letting go of something that can't be fixed.

I find this to be a fundamental misunderstanding with many quotes or articles I post about commitment. Someone always feels the need to chime in and tell me that if a relationship is abusive, then you should not stick around and try to make it work.

CHAPTER 3 NOW INCLUDES A CAMEO BY *CAPTAIN OBVIOUS.*

Commitment and "stick-to-itiveness" is all about understanding what types of situations will bring value to your life if they pan out, and what types of situations will hinder your progress. Oftentimes, if a relationship is so complicated that it needs to be specified as such by your Facebook relationship status, it should be abandoned on the side of the road and left to the wolves. Every relationship is going to have turmoil, conflict, disagreements, and fights — which is why we need to very carefully draw a line in the sand, right there.

Just because a relationship has fights does not mean it is a negative, non-constructive relationship. But, all negative relationships have fights. (What was that thing about a square being a rectangle, but a rectangle not being a square?) The issue arises when the person you're with ends up complicating your life more than they enhance it. When they make you feel lonely even when you are with them. When they make you feel discouraged or exhausted or beaten down emotionally. When they make you feel like you would rather be anywhere else — without them.

When you begin to draw these lines between negative feelings, and your partner, this is when a serious look at your relationship needs to happen. Are you trying to bail water out of a sinking ship? Are you simply switching seats on the

Titanic by trying to make it work ("this ship isn't going down, my end just rose fifty feet")? Are you trying to extinguish a fire with a squirt gun?

While there is levity in these analogies, there is absolutely nothing to joke about when it comes to a relationship that negatively impacts your life, in *any* way. Have the respect for yourself to walk away from anyone who makes you feel lonelier than when you were single.

CHAPTER FOUR
Judge a Book By its Cover (AND By its Content)

—

I hope you like the cover of this book, and I'm sure that Emily, the designer, hopes you like it too. But, as pretty as it is, books are not meant to be stagnant pieces of art that sit on your mantel or coffee table and are simply visually appealing. Ah, but! Some are...

Some books are fantastic coffee table pieces, and tend to generate a conversation simply by existing. Perhaps there is unique imagery on the cover, or maybe it is an interesting size; perhaps it is bold, or colorful, or abstract. Naturally, the question then becomes: *I wonder what's inside?*

Perhaps you pick up the book, flip it over, and read the back cover. This gives you a little more information, and helps you to determine whether you actually want to open it up and begin to peruse the pages. Maybe you ask a friend what they know about the book. Maybe you think about other books you've read that seem to be similar to this one, and begin to pull your conclusions by drawing on your own previous experiences.

Every single one of these methods brings you to the same exact destination though: *Knowing essentially nothing about what is actually inside, on those pages.*

I'm going to venture a guess and see if I can predict something about you that you wouldn't normally admit. It's okay, you can be honest — it's just you and me here.

You judge people, don't you? You judge people by the way they dress, the way they talk, the way they don't know which is the proper form of "your" to use (come on, people!) You judge people every single day for these little things, consciously or subconsciously — don't you? I know, I know, you really don't want to admit it, but it's just human nature.

We all grow up being told not to judge a book by its cover, yet we do it all day every day. We do it in business, we do it at the coffee shop, and we *absolutely sure as hell do it in dating.* Why do you think dating apps are so popular? Most people think that dating has gone to hell because of these apps that make us more judgmental and quick to swipe on people — both online and in real life. I, however, have a different theory.

I don't think dating apps have *caused* us to judge people quickly, I think they simply tapped into our basest human nature and gave us a way to indulge in our instincts privately. I think we enjoy swiping our way to oblivion because it's simply a transposition of what we do every single day, anyway. *Admit it, it's okay.*

You see someone walking in your direction at the bar out of the corner of your eye. So, you glance over. They're looking right at you. Eye contact. *Shit!* You immediately know you don't want to talk to him. Why? How? You know nothing about him — but you've already written him off.

You see a beautiful woman from across the bar. *Oh man, I have to talk to her.* You immediately start walking towards her because she's intrigued you. What? Why? You know nothing about her but the way she looks, but you're interested, for some reason.

It's because initial attraction and perception of another person is based strictly off of appearance. We don't like to admit it because it makes us sound shallow. Lucky for you, though, I'm the one saying it here. You simply get to nod along on the subway, on the bike at the gym, or wherever you're reading this book, and the people around you (who have already been subjected to your silent judgment) are none the wiser.

Now that we've established this reality of life, here's a

question for you: How many people have you gotten to know who have then surprised you? People who you talked to and said "Wow, that wasn't what I expected"? If we can keep this little tidbit of knowledge tucked away in the backs of our minds, it may help us give more people a chance, every now and then.

One of the things I enjoy about Los Angeles is the full spectrum of people who can be found in any given area at any given time. You will find a homeless person standing next to a billionaire in Beverly Hills. You will find a guy with every inch of his body covered in tattoos, at a restaurant with $100 steaks. You will find rock stars at small neighborhood coffee shops, and suburban moms at hipster bars. Everyone is free to be fully themselves, and nobody around really seems to notice or to care.

Why, though? It's not as if Los Angeles is some magical place where judgment doesn't exist. We can only imagine what might be going through the mind of the mother pushing the baby carriage past the dude in camo pants, a torn-up t-shirt, and a backwards hat (as she sees him hop into his exotic car, most likely), but that doesn't change the fact that people are coexisting in these environments.

My personal belief — which could be wrong — is that these people are happy being their genuinely selves (see Chapter 1), and therefore are unconcerned by what the other people around them are doing. Everyone is free to live their own lives in their own ways, and the more we can be secure in ourselves, the less we notice what others are doing in *their* own ways.

But, I think there's more to it than this. When we are around a more diverse collection of people, we actually interact with those who aren't like us. This happens with travel, moving to a new city, or simply going to a new part of town. And more often than not, we are pleasantly surprised that — gasp — they are human just like we are. They are trying to do their best: pay their bills, support their family, enjoy their life, just like you are. First impressions are certainly impactful, but they're not always accurate.

Human beings are multifaceted, and should be approached as such. Often times, we automatically find reasons to write someone off without actually getting to know them first. In doing so, we drastically reduce our chances of finding someone who ends up surprising us. I know plenty of people who complain about how "all men" or "all women" are the same, but when you look at their dating history, it makes you wonder whether or not cloning has been invented and you just missed the memo. If someone keeps following the same pattern, they're obviously going to end up with the same result.

This is why stepping outside of your comfort zone is important-- meeting new people, interacting with new crowds, getting to know different personalities. I'm not suggesting that the guy in the pink shirt and khakis is going to be a great match for Miss Goth City 2017, but hey, maybe they'll turn out to be compatible as friends. The point is, we need to be open to learning more about people past their appearance in order to determine whether or not they could be a potential match for us.

Consider these circumstances, *over and above appearance:*

What is the character of the people they are with?

You are the company you keep, no? It doesn't matter how friendly or clean cut or well put together someone may appear; if someone surrounds themselves with people who mistreat others or are generally rude and obnoxious, this reflects more on that person's character than their outward appearance does.

In the age of social media, it is easy to learn a lot about a person very quickly. The environments in which they spend their time and the people with whom they spend it will give you a glimpse into how they're choosing to live their lives. This is invaluable information that hints at long-term compatibility and can help you determine whether or not you'd like to get to know them more.

How does s/he treat their friends?

If you spend time around someone who is constantly gossiping and talking badly about others, you're left wondering how they talk about *you* when you're not around. It's one thing to tease your friends or poke fun at them for something innocent in casual conversation, but it's a whole other thing to criticize and ridicule people behind their back.

Kindness is not about being friendly when it's convenient to you or when the person your kindness is directed towards is right in front of your face. Truly genuine, kindhearted people, are consistent one hundred percent of the time because it's in their nature.

How do they treat the wait staff?

Very important. *Remember this—someone who is not nice to the waiter is not a nice person.* I make it an absolute point every single day in every interaction to show equal respect to everyone around me — if I'm the third person next to the homeless man and the billionaire in Beverly Hills, they're both getting a nod and a smile. Neither is superior in my eyes; both are human, and worthy of respect (until proven otherwise).

If you are out to dinner with someone, or simply observing them at a bar before deciding whether or not you want to talk to them, pay close attention to how they act towards those they are not trying to impress. I don't care how beautiful or well-dressed a woman is, if she emanates a negative attitude to the people around her, then I'm all set. For me, being social and friendly is a very important part of life, and if I'm going to be with a woman, I need to know that we can be in all types of situations together and she's not going to be rude to anyone. She should have the same confidence in how I will interact when she brings me into her circle, whether it is her friends, family, or a work event.

Whether you like it or not (if you don't like it, that's a red flag), the person you're with is a reflection of you. They send a message about the standards you set for yourself and the way you live your life. Having a kind heart is of utmost importance.

Paying close attention to these nuances is vital for a variety of reasons—not the least of which is that anyone can tell you anything you want to hear. Some people are extremely perceptive, will read you immediately, talk a big game, and present themself flawlessly in ways that will draw you to them. Sometimes, though, this is simply a facade for an underlying insecurity or a narcissistic nature. It's important to get an authentic view of this person relatively early on in your interactions.

If it's a man approaching you, how much effort is he dedicating toward getting to know *you*? Is he overly fixated on your looks? Is he making physical advances without gauging your comfort level? Is he suggesting you go somewhere for drinks, or is he putting more effort into spending time with you one-on-one, taking you out to dinner or picking up on cues from you and planning a date around your interests? It's important to get a better idea for what someone is genuinely like before simply agreeing to a date with him.

If it's a woman you've approached, has she already asked what you do for a living? Have you caught her fixating on your watch, or perhaps bringing up the type of car you drive? The "stereotypical" red flags for each gender are traditionally different from each other, but still have to be kept in the back of one's mind early on in your interactions. The idea is to learn about someone as a human being — and whether you are a man or a woman, focusing on surface or superfluous qualities, rather than an actual personality, is the ultimate red flag.

IF I SAID YOU HAD A NICE BODY, WOULD YOU HOLD IT AGAINST ME?

While there are variations in actual percentages, virtually every study you find on communication will tell you that the majority is nonverbal. That is, to say, body language. Particularly in intimate scenarios or settings that could lead to further intimacy, this is an important piece of the "first impression" puzzle.

How someone carries themselves and interacts with you in seemingly innocuous situations can give you clues to their interest level in you, their internal level of confidence, and even how real and genuine they are being in what they say to you. These are nuances that seem to get lost in this age of social media and online communication. We are so used to overanalyzing and deciphering tone from a text message *("Jenny, he just said "k"…do you think he's breaking up with me?!")* that we are losing our grip on what actual human interaction looks like beyond the surface.

Being observant is a simple yet rare art that can help to eliminate a lot of confusion while interacting with each other. Additionally, it can help us proactively communicate with others. If we can learn how to use body language to emphasize the point we are trying to make, or the message we are trying to convey, we can tap into a deeper level of connection that they will innately understand.

The simplest form of this I can think of is a smile or a nod. Imagine going to a foreign country where you do not know anyone, nor do you speak the language. If you smiled or nodded at someone passing by you in the street, you're utilizing a universally-understood gesture that most often results in comfort, or at least reciprocation. You did not have to learn to smile, nor did the person who grew up on the other side of the world. It is natural nonverbal human communication that we all *get*.

To get into more specific details regarding one-on-one interactions (particularly in a dating scenario), here are some widely accepted body language cues to be on the lookout for:

They're decreasing the distance between you

It may sound obvious, but if a person likes what you're saying or is feeling more comfortable with you, they will gradually move closer to you — whether it be angling their chair towards yours, leaning their shoulders in your direction, or repositioning themselves within a group for better proximity toward you. This is a subconscious cue that they're genuinely interested in you and what you're saying.

Conversely, if they're moving farther off, it's probably time to back off a bit.

They're subconsciously mirroring your movements

You'll find that people who are attracted to you tend to

mirror your movements subconsciously. They may become more animated if you are, or more subdued if you become calm. They will look to match your level of energy, tone of voice, or the speed at which you're talking. These are all good signs that someone is giving you their full attention and absorbing your presence, even if they don't even realize it.

They're positioned with their shoulders pointed squarely towards you

I played football and wrestled in high school, and one of the most important things we were taught to pay attention to is the center of a person's chest. Anyone can 'head-fake' you to think they're going one way when they're really going in the other, but if you watch where their core is going, that will tell you what you really need to know.

The same goes for body language when interacting with someone. If their feet and shoulders are pointed directly towards you, then you've got their full attention. If you notice that they are angled outwards or if they look like they are about to run off — then trust your intuition, because they probably are.

Back when I briefly did some coaching for men on how to approach women, a lot of what we would talk about was the importance of casually looking over your shoulder at her (picture: you're leaning on a bar facing the bartender, but looking at and focused on the woman next to you). This would keep the pressure off of her so you're not looming over her, but also give the impression that you're cool and casual (not that interested), which we all know can also serve the purpose of making you more attractive to the person you're "casually" interacting with Kind of cheesy, but hey, we all had to start somewhere.

They're standing with their arms open, loose, and relaxed

One need not be a body language expert to spot how tense someone looks if their arms are crossed tightly in front of their chest. It's a classic, instinctive pose used to protect yourself (you can make this symbolic about protecting your heart, if you'd like), and signals a lack of comfort towards the person you're facing. Once the arms come down, the guard typically comes down with them. This is a good way to know when to keep your distance, and when you're doing something right.

The ability to pick up on someone's nonverbal cues is an invaluable skill that can save you a lot of embarrassment (for example, by making a move when it's not welcome) and can also open the doors to new opportunities (by recognizing when someone is actually interested in you). I am certainly not a body language expert, but I have had enough social interactions over the years to be able to distinguish when someone is comfortable, and most importantly, when they're not.

For the men — it is impossible to emphasize enough how important this is. A woman's comfort should be your priority in every interaction. If she is not comfortable around you, she will certainly not trust you, which means she will certainly not be building on any initial attraction she may have harbored for you. Do not discount the importance of reading these cues. They will help you navigate the terrain—not only in dating, but in every other aspect of life as well.

CHAPTER FIVE

Project What You Want to Attract

—

I'll never forget my high school teacher who taught us that 'perception is reality' (shout-out to Mr. Coward, Arlington High School!) Over the years, I have learned how true this is in so many different areas of life, particularly when it comes to interpersonal relationships.

We spoke earlier about first impressions, and this is precisely where they originate. The way people perceive you will

govern the reality they create in their mind about you —
whether accurate or not. How you carry yourself and present
yourself will precede (and linger longer than) anything that
you say to someone. This is the unfortunate reality of life and
human nature (remember the dating app conversation earlier?).
This truth is just being magnified by the use of social media
and dating apps.

*It behooves us to ask ourselves then, are we really projecting
what we want to attract?*

I catch a lot of people talking about how they don't care
what other people think. When it comes to letting others in-
fluence how you live your life, that's a good mindset to have.
But, the reality is, how people perceive us will play a big role in
all different aspects of our lives, personally and professionally.

Someone's perception of you will affect whether or not
they hire you for a job. Whether or not they do business with
you. Whether or not they become friends with you. And —
absolutely — whether or not they date you. This perception is
determined by how you present yourself in person, but also

how you present yourself on social media. You know damn well that one of the first things someone is going to do when they learn your name is look you up online. What are they going to find?

I remember a few years ago when people would say things like "It's only Facebook, it's not real life." I would laugh and challenge them to insult someone on Facebook, and see if it gets brought up the next time you see them in person. *Social media is real life*. It is a transposition of the world onto a little screen where it all becomes condensed, segmented, and organized. We can choose which friends we want to observe from a distance, who we want to eliminate from our lives (I guarantee if you delete someone from your social media it's going to be awkward in person), and who we want to add into our lives.

People make a living off of endorsing products or services on social media. Instagram and YouTube stars are more recognizable in some arenas than television or movie stars. Doesn't this blow your mind? The point is that how you present yourself to the world, regardless of the medium or channel you're doing it through, *absolutely matters*.

Some things to consider here:

Yes, how you dress matters

I'm certainly not saying to dress in a certain style of cloth-ing or that you need to wear something you're uncomfortable with just to attract a certain type of man or woman, but the reality of the matter is that what you choose to wear will have people making assumptions about your personality before they even meet you.

Don't shoot the messenger.

Men and women are free to roam about, wearing their excessively distressed jeans or their tiny little skirts, with their bomber jackets and t-shirts, walking around in their sky-high heels or worn, ratty sneakers — nobody (especially me) is go-ing to tell you otherwise, nor would we have the right to. I can be found in my ripped jeans and a t-shirt just as often as the next guy — but I also won't go to dinner without a suit jacket, and I won't go to an event without wearing a dinner jacket or tuxedo. I make sure my online presence accurately depicts this versatility, and shows a true version of myself that aligns with how I want to be portrayed.

I understand that people are going to think certain things based on how I project myself to the world — both positive and negative. It's my responsibility to determine the most accurate way for me to show who I am. So while I am not telling you *how* you should dress and present yourself — I *am* telling you, drawing on decades of personal experience, that people are going to pay attention. So, choose wisely, and be sure your image is in line with what you want to attract.

Yes, where you spend your time matters

This may be the time when I start getting flak from some of you, but you've made it this far into the book by being able to handle the truth, so don't expect me to slow down now.If you want a serious relationship, do not portray yourself as someone who always likes to party. Again, I am telling you this from experience—people are going to judge you based on how you spend your time, and if there's a man or woman you're interested in who looks at your social media, they will either lose or gain interest in you, depending on what they see.

I used to post photos with a lot of different women when I was going out all the time. (If I do it now, it is from events, or shows, or being out with a group.) It used to be just because I wanted to be seen with beautiful people.

This was fun and would help my "street cred" until I'd meet a woman I was actually interested in, because then she would write me off as being a player. Whether or not that was true (at the time) is another book for another decade. The point is, you could be missing out on opportunities with great people if it doesn't look as though your lifestyle will mesh well with theirs. That's important in any relationship, and in a generation where the majority of social interactions begin through social media, judgments are going to be made about how you live your life.

I'm not saying it's fair, and I'm not saying it's right. I'm just saying that it's reality. If you are always out partying, or if you are always surrounded by members of the opposite sex, but you want someone who is stable, secure, and mature — you have to ask yourself if the ways you live your lives will align or not.

Quality over quantity

If your goal is to be seen as a man or woman who is ready to be in a monogamous, committed relationship, then your goal is no longer to attract the *most* men or women, it is to attract the *right* man or woman, and the way you act in your daily life should exude a level of maturity which reflects that.

I think back to my early... and mid... and part of my late... twenties, and consider all of the times that I was really only concerned with being around as many people as possible. How many women could I meet? How many phone numbers could I get? How many clubs could I visit in one single night? I had a newfound confidence after I had shed my previous skin, and was ready to take on the world. I had no interest in commitment or monogamy or building a relationship — so I lived my life in a certain way.

I dressed a certain way, I styled my hair a certain way (I may or may not have had a blonde mohawk for a while), and I definitely acted in a certain way. None of these things exuded the image of "boyfriend material." I do not regret those years because they helped to mold me into the person I am today, and they helped to teach me a lot about myself and about human interactions in general. However, I came to realize that if I wanted to live a serious life and be a mature adult man, I needed to change and adjust to begin living my life in a way that would reflect this desire.

As I changed the places I spent my time, and the people I surrounded myself with, I noticed drastic changes in the things that were happening around me.

The challenge to this: You are going to need to lose some people if you want to live your best life.

I think this is one of the biggest reasons why a lot of people find themselves stifled — they are unable to let go of those who are weighing them down. We are committed, loyal, even — to a fault. We are unwilling to enter the unknown, or to embark on a path where we cannot bring our entire entourage. But, at times, the entourage you have today will not be the one you have tomorrow.

And, sometimes, they may even be preventing you from finding happiness, or a partner to share your life with.

Do not get confused — I am not telling you to adjust your lifestyle for the sake of finding a partner, but what I am saying is that it may require some further introspection if you aren't willing to give up certain things that prevent you from finding a stable relationship. Dating isn't just about *finding* the right person; it's also about *being* the right person. Again, refer to the first chapter, here.

CHAPTER SIX

Have High Standards for Where You Spend Your Time *(and the people with whom you spend it)*

—

While we're on the subject…

Meeting and attracting the right people is not just about how it *looks* that you're living your life, it's about how you're *actually living it.*

I have coached women (ahem, same goes for the gents) who have told me that they never meet anyone new, but they can't figure out why. When this happens, it's always time for a little bit of forensic analysis [insert favorite crime drama theme song here]. The vast majority of the time, the conversation will go something like this:

Man/Woman: "James, where can I find all of these great men/women you write about? I never seem to meet anyone new."

JMS: "Well, what does your day-to-day usually look like?"

Man/Woman: "Well, I go to work in the morning, have lunch at my desk, and then I'm so tired after a long day I just go home at night."

JMS: WELL THEN, THAT EXPLAINS IT.

Consider this: We set forth a routine or a strategy to succeed in essentially every area of life. If we want to get a promotion, or a new job, or start a business — we set a goal and lay out the action steps for how to get there. We understand there are certain skills that may need to be acquired, or changes to the way we do things, or whatever the case may be.

If we want to get in better shape, we join a gym, or we start walking, running, or hiking. We change our eating habits. We adjust our routine and strategies based on our desired outcome.

What about dating? Getting into a relationship? We are told by our friends and family that "the right person just hasn't come along yet." *Bullshit! Utter bullshit!* This is lazy advice that does nobody any good. Mr. or Ms. Right isn't going to come knock on your door while you're finishing off that third carton of ice cream tonight, and they sure as hell aren't going to fall out of your office's panel-ceiling onto your desk inside of your cubicle.

Get off of your ass!

Dating is work. Meeting people is work. We need to be proactive about meeting new people on a consistent basis if we want to come across someone we may be able to build a relationship with. Put yourself into the places where you're most likely to be interacting with the people you're interested in. Are you passionate about serving your community? When was the last time you were at a charity event or a fundraiser? Do you have a creative side? Why not grab a friend by the hair and drag them to an art class? Does your dating profile say 'outdoorsy'? *That doesn't mean you like to drink on the patio!* Go on a hike and talk to people!

Here's something to try: Choose one day per week, and decide that you're going to go to a different restaurant for lunch that you've never tried before. Every week, choose somewhere new, and go spend some of your time there. Sit at the bar, chat up the bartender, talk to people around you. Make new friends. You will be shocked at how quickly your social circle begins to grow. It's just a matter of getting out there and being proactive.

Think about it: your life is merely the product of *who* you spend the most time with, and *where* you are spending this time. It might be easy or comfortable to stay in the same routine, to go to the bar around the corner for happy-hour on Friday. To just order takeout and binge-watch TV shows this weekend instead of getting dressed up. To hit *snooze* in the morning instead of getting up early to go to the gym. All of these things live within your comfort zone.

BUT NOTHING GREAT EVER COMES FROM STAYING IN YOUR COMFORT ZONE.

And, the people you *want to meet* are certainly not snuggled up in there with you. Guys, you've got to say hello to more women. Be friendly. Smile. Take that rejection on the chin. Do it again. And again. And again. Ladies, smile at that handsome hunk of man-meat across the room and see if he'll approach you. Say hello to someone in line at the coffee shop. Do something different than you normally do, maybe even a little bit outside of your immediate comfort zone.

Men and women pass by each other all day every day, and then get to their desk or their couch or their bed and write on

Facebook about how there are no good men or women left in the world — besides — of course, the ten thousand of them you passed by during the course of your day but didn't talk to, because you've already made up your mind that no one is worthy.

It is difficult to step out of your comfort zone and risk rejection, but nothing in your life will ever change until you do. Ask yourself: What's worse, pushing yourself to break the pattern you're in now, or actually *staying in the pattern you're in now?*

This is one of the absolute biggest challenges that we face in dating and relationships — breaking out of our shells and taking a new approach towards meeting people, when it might make us initially uncomfortable. It's going to feel this way because this step requires you to change your routine, go new places, talk to people you've never met — *but that's entirely the point.*

I remember reading a study a few years ago that said something along the lines of the average person doesn't leave a seven-mile radius on a daily basis. When you consider average commute distances, this makes sense. Most people go from home, to work, to the gym, to home, rinse, repeat. It's natural that we are going to have a hard time meeting new people if we don't break these patterns.

When I coach a new client, the very first thing we talk about is how many new people they are meeting on a regular basis. The answer is usually close to zero, and it becomes easy to find ways to expand their horizons during their day-to-day routines. All this requires is a little outside perspective.

You are the only person who can control the path of your life and decide to break the cycle you've found yourself in. But, that doesn't mean other people aren't going to be involved.

TAKE INVENTORY OF YOUR LIFE

—

It's important to take an honest assessment of the people you're surrounding yourself with:

> *Are they on the same life path as you?*
>
> *Do they have the same level of ambition as you?*
>
> *Do they have the same relationship status as you?*
>
> *Are they making you a **better** version of yourself?*

It's important to be honest about how you're being affected by those you're spending the most time with. These are the people from whom we tend to pull the most energy, and therefore become more like. It is often said that you become like the top five people you spend your time around, so it is easy to see that you can fall into patterns if they are people who are, perhaps, in relationships and are happiest just spending time on the couch with their spouse.

Perhaps your top five are less social than you, and just want to go home after work. Perhaps they are *too* social, and spend every night out at the bar until two AM. Maybe, just maybe, these people are not truly *your tribe.* It's hard to let go people, but losing someone who is dragging you down and holding you back in life is not really a significant loss.

Take this inventory of your life and envision the relationship you want to have. Can you picture living your life in its current state, and also finding that relationship? Finding that man or woman, and having them fit into your lifestyle, as it currently exists? Could that man or woman come around your friends and be comfortable?

IF THE ANSWER TO ANY OF THESE QUESTIONS IS *NO*, THEN YOU'VE GOT TO ASK YOURSELF: *WHAT NEEDS TO CHANGE?*

Then, you need to have the courage and strength to actually change it. Taking this inventory is not for fun, it is for a purpose: A way to identify a better path to turn down in order to find what you want. If you don't actually make the changes, then what is the point of putting in any effort at all?

It may require you spending some time socially alone, going to events or new places by yourself. I personally love doing this — I go out all the time by myself. Whether it is to get coffee, or dinner, or to higher profile events, I have no problem at all flying solo. In fact, I find it fun and exciting, because you never know what's going to happen.

When you are out on your own, you never know who you might meet, or where the evening may take you. You could find yourself chatting up a chap at the bar who stumbled upon the event on his way home from work. Perhaps you bump into a pretty little lass picking up your car at the valet. Who knows what could happen. The point is, you need to *be where the people are.*

BE SAFE, BE AWARE OF YOUR SURROUNDINGS, BE SMART — BUT BE SOCIAL.

CHAPTER SEVEN

Playing the Numbers Game

—

I am pretty open about my theory that dating is a numbers game. This may be controversial, but I am here to spark a conversation into action, so let's get to it!

My personal belief is that you need to experience relationships with a wide range of people that teach you what you what you *don't* want, before you can fully appreciate the person that embodies the qualities that you *do* want. I understand that there are situations where high school sweethearts fall in love, mature together, never date anyone else, and end up married with beautiful families — and I think that is absolutely fantabulous when it happens. I also think it is very rare, and sometimes ends in heartache because one (or both) teammates did not take the time to learn what they actually wanted out of life.

Now, don't slam this book shut and throw it in the fire just yet; hear me out. I know of a lot of people who have been together since a young age that end up parting ways in their middle-aged years (or sooner), because they never "played the field" so to speak. *I am not advocating that you run around and pull your pants down (or your skirt up) for anything that has two legs, but, hell, who am I to judge.*

What I am saying is that I have found healthy relationships are often built on a foundation of experience, between two people who had previously been with others that didn't end up being their life partner, and they learned lessons from these relationships. Refer to chapters two and three, about defining what you do and don't want. How are you going to do that if you don't actually *know* what you do and don't really want? How many times have you gotten something you wanted, looked at it, and thought: *This isn't all it's cracked up to be.*

It is absolutely vital to your happiness in the long term (*remember the disclaimer: this is my personal opinion*) that you date a variety of people before you can fully decide what type of person you'd like to spend the rest of your life with, let alone narrow it down to who it's actually going to be. I had a series of years in my early... to mid... even all the way through my late-ish twenties where I wanted nothing to do with commitment. I had a newfound confidence, a great group of friends, and I wanted to fly free. So that's exactly how I spent my time.

I am absolutely a more mature, grounded, better person because of it. I understand myself better, and I understand women better. I understand what I do want in a relationship, and what I am able to give to and bring to the table within a relationship. Had I not had the experiences that helped me learn and grow, I would be spinning my wheels and getting nowhere.

Let me reiterate: I am not encouraging you to date every single person who comes along. The idea here is to attract quality, not quantity. But — ideally — a quantity *of* quality. And, that means being selective about with whom you spend your time.

I'm not a gambler, but I am a chronic user of analogy. Picture walking into a casino and having one hundred dollars in your pocket. Are you going to take that hundred dollars and put it all down on the first table you see? Absolutely not — what if you lose? You will be heartbroken, and have go to home, and probably cry. But what if you took small portions and spread it across multiple different tables? Then, you could determine which ones you did and didn't like, which ones suited you best, and which ones you wanted to cut off quickly.

This allows you to be less caught up at one table, and keep your wits about you as you determine which is the best fit. Eventually, you notice one table treating you better than all the rest, and you begin to invest more and more, until you're "all in."

During this time, of course, you're going to be pursued by other dealers at the other tables who will all want a piece of your action. This goes for both men and women, because people want what they can't have. It's about scarcity. Supply and demand. There's only one of you, but there are a million of them. Who's going to get your attention?

This goes back to chapter one, and recognizing your own value. If you walked into an exotic car dealership with a few dollars in your pocket, no amount of negotiating would get you out the door with that car. Why? Because the car has an intrinsic value that doesn't have to be proven to the person who can afford it. There are people out there who can and will pay this price, and will eventually walk through the door and put their money where their mouth is.

You see, the car has enough worth to know that it doesn't have to compromise itself. Eventually, the right person will come in and make the investment.

Oh, look, another analogy.

CHAPTER EIGHT

Wave The White Flag
When You See *These* Red Flags

—

Hey, you...*pssst*...you're a fixer, aren't you? You find yourself in consistent patterns of dating people you think you can help, or fix, or change, or that you just know you will finally be the one for, the one who makes them see the light and fix the errors of their ways, right? How often does that actually work out for you?

If you're anything like, let's see, the *vast majority* of the population, then you're tired of being blindsided by people who weren't actually what or who they claimed to be. One thing I find interesting though, is when someone tells me that "he or she changed" early on into the relationship.

Sorry — no — they didn't change. They simply revealed who they truly were after they were tired of putting on an act in order to get your attention. Now, I'd be lying if I said you'd be able to spot a toxic man or woman one hundred percent of the time before it's too late. But you can arm yourself with the necessary mental equipment to potentially spot some warning signs and save yourself some time, energy, and a lot of inevitable heartache.

For that reason, I've compiled a list of these warning signs to look for, right here.

—

They are always the victim.

Someone who is always painting themselves as a victim in life and in specific situations is likely unable to accept responsibility for their own actions, and therefore work to improve their shortcomings. This person will always be looking to point the finger when a problem arises, and if it's a problem in your relationship, guess who the finger will be pointed at?

Consider concepts I have spoken about earlier in this book—about growing, learning, and developing from facing challenges and failures. Now, consider someone who is fundamentally incapable of doing just that. They will continue to live their lives as if the world is out to get them, they will find it difficult (or impossible) to apologize — why should they when nothing is their fault — and they will not be able to properly pull their weight as your teammate because they'll be too busy complaining about how things are not going their way.

I understand that some people do have it tough, and I fully believe partners in a relationship should support and lift each other up. But we must be aware of when someone creates problems for themselves and consistently places themselves squarely in victimhood. This is not a pattern that can be broken by an outside source (you).

They are controlling.

A person who tries to control their significant other in a relationship is likely lacking the confidence to believe that they can attract a romantic partner and subsequently keep their attention. In order to make up for this, they do their best to control the situation so there are no surprises. Needless to say, this can only lead to you feeling suffocated and restricted – two things you should never feel in a relationship.

One of my LEAST favorite quotes about relationships (I think I have read every one to ever exist) is "the person who cares less has the power." I think this is total and utter hogwash, rubbish, fuckall, bullshit--whatever term you'd like to throw at it.

Relationships are not about control, nor about power. Relationships are not about one partner having the upper hand

over the other and forcing them (consciously or subconsciously) to constantly fight for approval because they don't feel worthy of it. These are classic control tactics and should cause you
to head for the hills in the fastest car you can hijack from your
neighbors.*

*I am not actually encouraging or condoning
Grand Theft Auto, in case that's unclear.

They are desperate.

If someone is constantly seeking your approval or trying to
jump into a relationship with you quickly, it is a warning sign
that they are unable to be on their own and require a significant other in life in order to be "happy." They have not yet
worked to developed the emotional maturity in order to be
happy with themselves first, and therefore will never be truly
happy in a relationship.

Consider the first chapter of this book, and all we talked
about, that goes into developing yourself into the person that
you have always wanted to become. It is a lifelong journey, and
that is the beauty of it. To find someone who is also on this

journey and shares in it with you (both as an individual and as a team) is the jackpot, in my opinion. Consider, then, the difficulty in building a relationship with someone who has not even started down this path that you have been walking along for years. It may be through no fault of their own, but your compatibility as a pair over the long term is drastically depleted if you do not share in this passion for self-improvement, or self -discovery.

A GOOD TEST? IF THEY ARE NOT INTERESTED IN THIS BOOK, DON'T DATE THEM.
JUST KIDDING. KIND OF. (NOT.)

Of course, someone new should be enthusiastic about being with you. Dating should be fun and exciting, and you should be enjoying every moment of each other's company. This is why it's important to be sure that the excitement is genuine and comes from a place of preexisting fulfillment. Someone who is seeing a reflection of their whole self in *you* — another *whole person*. Not someone who is looking for you to complete them, because this will inevitably end in disaster as they become more dependent on you over time in order to validate their self-worth.

Self-worth is called *self-worth* for a reason, because it's supposed to come from within you.

They are always involved in drama.

Someone who always seems to be surrounded by drama or chaos is unlikely to have it just… following them around. The term "common denominator" comes to mind; if they are always in the middle of conflict, it is probably a product of them. When this person enters into a relationship with you they are not going to suddenly lose the characteristics that create this tension. They will bring it to you and try to take you into it with them.

Think about someone you know who always seems to be caught up in some nonsense. Their social media feed reads like the docket on a civil court parody show. Eventually, I'd bet they end up getting less and less attention from the people around them, because it's friggin' exhausting. Unfollow that, thanks.

Now, imagine actually dating that person. If you've ever been with someone like this, you can understand how emotionally draining it is to live inside of a soap opera. Some people simply feed off of this type of lifestyle, perhaps because they have had a pattern of tumultuous relationships, or grew up in a similar environment. I am certainly not qualified to give anyone a psychiatric evaluation, but it certainly seems to me that some people are so comfortable living in conflict, that if they don't have it happening around them — they look for ways to create it.

Run away from these people.

They are perpetually sarcastic.

Sarcasm and wittiness can be funny, and even attractive if inserted into a conversation appropriately. But when it permeates every conversation and there is always an underlying tone that seems to be condescending, this person will become increasingly difficult to have an actual discussion with as time goes on, particularly about important issues. Your partner in a relationship should have the emotional depth and security to leave the sarcasm at the door when necessary.

I find that some people these days wear their sarcasm as a badge of honor. They almost enjoy being seen as unaffectionate, or abrasive. This has never sat well with me — I don't think it makes you look stronger, or cooler, or more desirable than anyone else. I don't think it's sexy. I don't think it's cute. I don't think you get extra bonus points because you have an attitude.

It is impossible to build a genuine bond with someone who keeps every person they meet at an arm's length. I believe that this self-distancing is a type of defense mechanism that prevents someone who's been hurt in the past from being hurt again — but really, this simply speaks to an inner battle on their part that needs to be overcome before one can build a strong connection with someone else. Of course, this is a generality, but in my experience it rings true the majority of the time.

To me, a relationship should be a soft, affectionate, genuine experience between two people. Those who are too "prickly" so to speak, don't invite a kind, genuine heart. Some men and women these days remind me of hugging a porcupine. Thank you for the offer, but... no.

They never seem to give you a straight answer.

Simple questions only require simple answers. If you find that someone is always avoiding discussions or topics that actually matter in your relationship (or even ones that don't really matter), they are either hiding something or are unable to have this type of conversation. Both should be warning signs.

Open and honest communication is a nonnegotiable building block of any relationship, whether it be intimate or otherwise. If you cannot trust someone to give you their truth when it comes to something small, how can you possibly trust them to do it when something serious arises? How can you possibly express yourself openly with someone that you do not fully trust? How can you *love* someone you don't fully trust?

How can you *rely* on someone that you can't fully trust?

People who avoid important topics will never be able to help you build the foundation that is required for a strong relationship. This foundation cannot be built by one person.

They don't really listen to you.

Speaking of open and honest communication – it has to go both ways in order to be effective. If someone consistently speaks far more than they listen (especially in conversations about your wants or needs), then it is a warning sign that they could be self-centered or even narcissistic. Not desirable qualities in a romantic partner.

I hear this far too often (no pun intended)-- someone is consistently feeling like they're not truly being *heard* in a relationship. I believe that teammates in a relationship should be able to express their frustrations, desires, wants, and needs to each other without ever having to experience the fear of being judged. This is how we can learn about each other, into the most intimate corners of our hearts and minds. This is how we can understand what makes our partner the most happy, and adjust accordingly. This is how we know what to plan for date night, what food to cook, what vacation spots to go to, how they like their coffee in the morning.

This is also how we know what bothers our partner, even if it's something small that we can actively put effort into stopping. Communication is how we can mold our relationships to be the best possible experience for both people involved. Someone who cannot listen to you and absorb what you say to them will never be able to be an equal teammate to you, or for anyone else.

They are constantly talking badly or spreading rumors about other people.

As Eleanor Roosevelt famously said, "great minds discuss ideas; average minds discuss events; small minds discuss people."

I feel that it is vital to be able to engage in deep,

meaningful conversations with the person you've partnered with. Relationships are not built on the surface, they are built through a bond with another human being that is unique to you both. A bond that recognizes and is enhanced by your individual nuances, dreams, desires, and personality traits. A bond that celebrates the similarities, and respects the differences. When two separate, unique individuals come together as one, they will interact and connect in a way that no other combination of two human beings ever will. This is why staying hopeful after breakups is important, because everyone is different. But, that's for another conversation.

Some people seem to be constantly caught up in the soap opera of the lives around them: the gossip, the surface-level chatter that doesn't move the world (or your relationship) forward at all. These things do not help you connect or learn more about each other, because the topic of conversation is focused around other people.

It's important for someone to be curious about the world; it's part of being your own individual person to have distinct goals, dreams, desires, ambitions, passions. If he or she is always worried about how everyone else is living their lives, they may not be able to work with you to build one of your own together.

They are never wrong.

Different than the above point about accepting responsibility for their actions – toxic people also refuse to change their opinions based on the presentation of new information or ever admit that they are wrong about something. This prevents them from growing intellectually and emotionally because they think they already know everything, so what's left to learn? Equally important though, it prevents you from having meaningful communication with them (are you seeing a pattern here?).

I don't know about you, but I actually enjoy being wrong... sometimes. It provides me with an opportunity to learn something new, and grow as a person. Plus, relationships require compromise. They require discussion. Collaboration. *Teamwork.* And if someone is convinced that they are always right, or have all of the answers, then everything is always going to have to be done their way.

Believe me, this is no way to build a relationship. I've been face-to-face with it before. If everything you do feels wrong because your partner's way is the only right way, then this person is not going to magically soften up one day and realize the importance of compromising with you. Be sure you are honest with yourself about how flexible you are being. There's a big difference between bending for another person and stretching yourself so far that you're breaking for them. Especially if they don't bend for you in return.

They are constantly exaggerating.

This may not seem like much of a warning sign when compared to my other points, but a person who has difficulty accurately representing reality and has an innate need to make themselves and their experiences sound more profound or better than they really are intrinsically lacks the self-esteem and integrity needed in order to be honest. How can you build a relationship with someone whose truth and honesty you are always questioning? You can't. Start thinking of exaggerating as a form of lying, and it may present itself as a bigger red flag.

Plus, it's easy to see how this could potentially be tied to narcissism (again, I am not providing any diagnoses here), but if you always have to be the biggest, baddest, strongest, fastest, hottest, or most of something — chances are you are too focused on your own image to effectively contribute to another person's emotional well-being in a relationship.

The team that a relationship is, is about building each other up. Supporting each other. Sharing the spotlight. Sharing responsibilities. Understanding that neither is better or worse than the other. Sharing equal respect. How can you possibly do this with someone who always has to be the best at everything—even when it means besting their partner at every turn?

You can't.

You're always the one going back.

The frequent pattern of breaking up and getting back

together is by itself a huge red flag and (hopefully) obviously unhealthy for any relationship. When you're the one always running back and the only one apologizing, it's a bad sign that things are turning toxic. Healthy relationships are about compromise and taking responsibility for your role in each and every miscommunication and disagreement.

If someone is not fighting to keep you, do not do them the honor of taking up any more of your time, body, or heart. Only give these things to people who have earned them—and continue to put in the same effort daily.

CHAPTER NINE

If You Have No Expectations, You Will Be Disappointed

—

Have you ever heard someone say that if you don't expect anything from people, you'll never be disappointed? Next time you hear someone give you this advice, kindly tell them to purse their little mouth closed so no more words of such nonsense can pour out into the already-polluted universe.

Chapter Nine

You absolutely should have expectations for people, particularly in relationships. They are otherwise known as standards, and without them, you can very easily fall into a pattern of being mistreated, or carelessly tossed aside, by many of the people you encounter.

If someone fails to meet your expectations, yes, you may be disappointed, but it also brings up an opportunity for conversation. Perhaps they weren't aware of your expectations, perhaps they don't know *how* to meet them, but *are willing to*, and just need a little bit of help. But, if we stop setting expectations for someone's code of conduct, then we devolve into the wild wild west, where anything goes.

In this ninth chapter, if we'd spent all of this time talking about how to spot warning signs, setting standards, developing your self-worth, and surrounding yourself with higher quality people, what kind of message would it send if we reinforced the idea that "if you don't expect things from people, you'll never be disappointed"? The truth is, if you never expect things from people, you will *always* be disappointed, because you'll never be sending the message that you actually have standards.

And you will definitely not find the person willing and able to rise to meet them.

This is the precise moment in time where the standards you have built for yourself really come into play. It's not just about how you want other people to act, but it's about how you act as well. How do you respond to people to let them know what you do, or don't expect from them? How do you communicate this to people in the way you live your life? Are you holding yourself to the same standards with which you measure other people?

And if so, how are you making that known?

Remember — you can't control other people, but you can control what you tolerate from other people. You have the power and the ability to walk away from any situation that is harmful to you, emotionally, and *absolutely* physically.

It's important to understand that you are actively conditioning people around you in how you should be treated based on how you treat yourself. What expectations do you hold for yourself? What standards do you hold for yourself? How do you project yourself? How do you carry yourself? What kinds of people are you surrounding yourself with?

Ah, did I just *Miyagi* you? *(Google that one, Millennials).* Have I been bringing all of these concepts full circle to help you create a well-rounded image of how you want to project yourself to the world in order to attract the type of love that you actually deserve? I'm not sure if I'm quite that smart, but that certainly feels like that's where this is headed, doesn't it?

Perhaps the best method we have for communicating what we expect from others is showing them what we expect from ourselves. However, that doesn't mean that we don't need to give an extra nudge in the right direction now and then.

A few important concepts for expressing your standards in a relationship:

Do not be demanding or mean.

Nobody likes to be told what to do, or ordered around *(except maybe in the bedroom, wink wink)*. But let's save the ultimatums for hostage negotiations, shall we? Nobody should ever be made to feel like they have entered into a boss/employee scenario when they're speaking with their significant other. I see a lot of people online who set ground rules for what they will and won't accept — which in theory, is fine. But, in practice, it usually comes across like a checklist for what *not* to do.

Hi, my name is Steve/Cindy/Nicole/Michael, and this is my online dating profile. I absolutely can't stand people who talk with food in their mouth. I hate baseball. If you don't watch Game of Thrones, please swipe left. If you can't tell me who was King of England in 1309, I don't want to have babies with you. But — I'm super easygoing, totally friendly, and would love to get together for a vegan grass-fed matcha iced tea with almond milk and chat with you about my existential crises!

Eye. Roll.

Chapter Nine

We spend far too much time talking about what we *don't* want, and not nearly enough empowering the things that we *do want* to come into our lives. Be positive, uplifting, proactive, optimistic. Show people that you are going to be fun to plan a date with, and that it's not going to feel like running errands or doing chores. Dating should be *fun*. It should be a mutually enjoyable experience where two people can thrive off of each other's energy and not want the evening to end (ahem, that's how you get a second date). If all we have to go off is what the person *dislikes*, then how are we supposed to expect to enjoy the experience?

It doesn't take more than a few minutes of scrolling through social media comments or review websites to notice a glaring trend in human nature: We tend to focus on the negative. We spend a lot of time writing scathing reviews about how our French fries were horrible at the latest fast food joint, but we don't seem to have the same zest for talking about how phenomenal the young man or woman was behind the counter when we voiced our complaint in person (did we even bother to do that?).

I hear of people now and then pledging to take challenges where they refuse to complain about anything for thirty days. Can you imagine? *Oh, the humanity!*

But what happens when you do something like this (even for thirty *minutes*) is you stop focusing on the things you *don't* want, and start focusing on the things you *do* want. And very often, we begin to find more positivity following us around that way. This goes for all areas of life, not just dating.

FOCUS.

Consider this: Have you ever heard a news report about someone driving along a desolate, deserted road but somehow ending up crashing into the only tree or telephone pole in sight? How do they manage that? We notice these things when we really start to pay attention in life. I mean put in the effort to become truly aware of your surroundings and day-to-day activities. You move toward what you focus on – just like driving or racing a car, you need to focus on where you want to go, not where you don't want to go. Your mind will steer you in the direction of your goals.

How many times do we all have something bad happen to us, and we focus on it like crazy? As the old saying goes "when one door closes, another opens – but we stare so long at the closed door we don't see the new one open." How true though. We're all guilty of it, even though we just as often realize it's extreme self-sabotage.

If everyone reading this was innately aware of how powerful his or her thoughts and focus are, I'm confident you'd never have another negative thought again. Your mind will steer you where you need to go – the challenge is having the constant fortitude to not become mired in or avoid altogether negative thoughts or situations. Positivity and passion are the fuel of progress and you always need to keep your tank full.

There is too much negative out in the world that we all come in contact with on a daily basis. People are miserable and it's socially acceptable. If you're happy for no reason, it's "weird." The news is all negative. When was the last time something truly positive and inspiring was reported? Maybe for ten seconds of puff on a slower day.

We need to find that balance. While we need to be informed of and educated on what's going on in the world if we can ever hope to enact real change, we also need to be always be feeding our mind with positive fuel if we expect to get anything positive out of it.

Am I saying it's easy or that I have mastered this task? Absolutely not. I am just as susceptible to those depressing days or letting my mind run away from me as the next person – maybe even more so. But I do my best to always remember that every single situation every day, no matter how big or small, provides me with a choice to create my own quality of life.

There is a scene in a movie called "About Time" which I highly recommend. In the movie, a man has the ability to go back in time (it sounds cheesy, but trust me it's not), and takes a life lesson from his father who encourages him to live every day as he normally would, but then go back to the start of it and focus on all of the small pleasures in life that he missed the first time around.

On his second trip through the day, he finds himself noticing the beautiful architecture of the room he rushed through before. He is nodding along to the music being played far too loud by the man on the train – which was an annoyance before. He is stopping, smiling, and quite literally smelling the roses.

The movie is inspirational, but it also prompts reflection. Reflection on the fact that unlike this character, we aren't granted the opportunity to travel back in time and live the day over. We get one chance. One shot. One time around. Every single day.

The quality of our thoughts really does govern the quality of our lives. Are we going to focus on how far we have come, or how far we have to go? Our failures, or our successes? What we wish we had, or what we already do have?

What could have been, or what already is?

Happiness is a choice, but it's not just a choice we can

make one time and expect to last. We have to choose happiness all the time, every day. You can either (choose to) view this as a burden or as an opportunity. I believe we can easily recognize who has made which choice with a quick look around.

This is certainly not a book about accepting how things are. Chasing after your goals takes a relative level of discontent. The willingness to want and obtain more. To be more, to do more, to contribute more. There is no progress in comfort, but that doesn't mean that you can't earn some opportunities to simply enjoy the journey along the way. After all, isn't that all we really have? The journey.

I know a man who always talks about the importance of "the dash." The dash, the small etched line on a stone that will eventually represent all of us, forever. That small dash between two numbers, two years. But it's not really just a dash, is it? *It's a life. It's a series of accomplishments. It's tears, and laughter, and love. It's a family. A legacy. A chance to make it so much more than that.*

What that dash really means is up to you, that's one of the great things about it. The other great thing about it is that you've never quite missed your chance to make it what you want. You get to decide every second of every day. And what you decide will ultimately determine who you attract.

Compromise.

My goodness. Compromise is not a dirty word, I promise you. Being willing to compromise, and not planting a stake in the ground to mark your ultimatums, is an absolutely invaluable approach to making both partners in a relationship happy. I know, I know, this should absolutely not even have to be said — but unfortunately — here we are.

It has to be said, because our society has started to turn inwards on itself. By that, I mean that we are so caught up in our own image, our own success, our own identity, that we are becoming accustomed to having things *our own way*. And when we *don't* get our way, we simply move on to another situation where we can make it happen, maybe with less effort and energy exerted.

This is not how relationships work. Compromise (and some-times, yes, sacrifice) is a reality of life that you need to accept if you're going to be in any kind of relationship. If you enjoy being single and don't intend on finding a life partner — which, by the way, is totally fine — then you can disregard this section and continue on reading about improving yourself and setting standards. But, for those of you who are actively look-ing for a relationship, you need to understand that compromise is the key.

Forgive me for saying this, but I do believe this is a bigger issue for the younger generations who have grown up fully immersed in their own worlds of social media. I am a big fan of social media, and without it, you probably wouldn't be read-ing this book right now. But the fact of the matter is that if we allow it to dictate how we live our lives and view our own self-worth *(how many likes did I get today?)* then we are never going to be able to step outside of ourselves into a situation where we are not always the most important person in the room. Other-wise referred to as a healthy relationship.

Teamwork makes the dream work.

If you know me, you know it's an absolute miracle that I've made it this far into the book without using this hackneyed yet absolutely true maxim. Teamwork really does make the dream work, and the best teams come together when each member knows what is expected of them.

The great thing about teams is that each person involved is typically better at certain things than the others. This is what creates a synergy. A harmony, based on expectations and roles that are established, taking into account each individual's strengths.

Now, before the book gets tossed into the fire again, I am not suggesting that we reinforce traditional gender roles. This book did not come with an apron for the women, and a hammer for the men. What I am suggesting is that each individual team figures out what works best for them. I, personally, enjoy cooking very much. A "traditionally female role," which I would be happy to take on in a relationship. I am not suggesting you fall into roles that society has dictated, I am suggesting that you recognize the strengths, interests, and natural skills of each person in the relationship, and use them as guidelines for who can be expected to do what.

Are both of you good at the same things? Great! Take turns! Or, do it together and become even better at it! It doesn't have to be a black and white line drawn in the sand; it's about fluidity and mutual support. *TEAMWORK MAKES THE DREAM WORK.*

I believe that we have reached a societal turning point where we need to be honest about the fact that one person does not have to do everything alone in order to be considered a success. Why has "help" turned into a dirty word? Why must we be completely autonomous in order to feel strong? Why is it that we spread ourselves too thin and automatically associate being *busy* with being *productive*?

Do you think I could put together this whole book by myself? I don't know how to design a cover, I don't know how to design a website, I don't know how to produce a profession- al video. Hell, you might be reading this saying, "*This guy doesn't even know how to write!"* The point is, I understand that needing people with skillsets different from mine does not diminish the (limited) skillsets that I do possess. It simply magnifies them by allowing them to shine through the proper channels in the proper ways.

The same concept goes for a relationship. When my grandfather was alive, he would joke about his "50/50" cooking arrangement with my grandmother. *"She cooks it, I eat it!"* he would say. A sure sign of the times they grew up in, but if we can pull apart the concept, perhaps there are lessons to be learned.

He would work constantly, and in an era where women were limited in their professional opportunities, it was necessary for the man to bust his ass every day to provide for his family. Some people still find this to be the most effective strategy for them. In other circumstances, the woman will be the breadwinner. In still others, there is an equal financial contribution. It completely depends on *what works for the specific relationship at hand.* There is no better or worse. There is no right or wrong. We need to be careful about falling into what

society tells us is traditional, if it's not what works for us *as
individuals.*

This is yet another reason why communication between
partners is so important. We have to be careful of making assumptions about how someone wants to live their life when
they are single, as compared to dating, and finally as compared
to being married. Anytime either my brother or I would start
to get serious with a woman we were dating (hell, even the first
time she would meet the family), our grandfather would cut
right to the chase:

*"So, if you have kids, you'll quit your job and stay home with them,
right?"*

Boy, did that ruffle some feathers and make for some
clean-up work for Blake and me. *Don't worry, my grandfather's
viewpoints are not representative of the whole family.* Our disclaimer was prepared and presented ahead of time.

The point is, though, that different things work for

different people, in different generations. Norms we are settling into right now may be completely uprooted when we are all grandparents (if we even have kids and they even have kids). We scoff at how previous generations did things, as they likely did to those before them, who likely did to those before them. The point is, if it worked, it worked. It's up to us now to find what works for us.

Constructive criticism.

Who likes to be criticized? Uh, *nobody.* That said, constructive guiding criticism, can help someone learn and improve, particularly when it comes to making their significant other happy (which should always be a priority). Like anything else in life, it's not *what* you say, it's *how* you say it.

When it comes to expressing expectations, how you approach your partner is of the utmost importance. Of course, this is going to change on a case-by-case basis, and will depend on the personality type of the person you're interacting with, how long you have been together, the issue at hand, as well as a whole slew of other circumstances. But regardless of the individual situation, I have found one common mantra to be the most effective:

Do not focus on what they're doing, focus on how it makes you feel.

Let's say, for example, they've adopted their twelfth puppy and your bed is starting to get a bit crowded. You want to encourage them to stop adopting puppies, but what's the best way to go about it?

"I really hate it when you keep bringing puppies home, Steven," is probably not the best approach.

Try something more like:

"You know, Susan, I'm starting to feel a little overwhelmed by having all of these puppies here."

What's happening during this shift of perspective is that you are expressing to your partner that their actions have a certain negative impact on how you are made to feel as directly influenced by them. You are making the same statement (except, who would hate twelve puppies?), but you are framing it in a way that should be able to make them understand how what they're doing is hurting you.

"I really can't stand it when you come home late at night without calling," will be received much differently than *"You know, it makes me really worried when I don't hear from you for a while after work."*

Same message, different framing. And any man or woman who deserves to be in a relationship with you will never want to act in ways that purposefully hurt your feelings. You are effectively setting your expectations (standards) by communicating in this manner, and you are drastically increasing your chances that your partner — or *whoever you're talking to* — is going to positively respond. This goes for all other areas of life, as well.

I had a phone call with a client once who expressed her theory that the majority of failed relationships are a result of unmet expectations — which subsequently is a result of un-*communicated* expectations. Many times, we end up in a relationship with someone and just make assumptions that they are going to have the same perspective(s) as us, or that they are going to magically develop telepathic powers that spell out our thoughts to them on a holographic billboard that constantly floats above our heads as we meander throughout our day.

Or, something like that.

Alas, though, we probably have a few more years of technological advancement before we reach the era of personal holographic billboards designed directly from brainwaves. Until then, we are going to have to rely on good ol' fashioned communication. Communication of expectations, communication of disapprovals, communication of *love, respect,* and *honesty.*

And, we have to be cognizant of the fact that we cannot simply lay out ground rules once and expect for our communication duties to be complete for the duration of the relationship. This is a daily venture requiring consistent effort, hence, our arrival at the final chapter (not as ominous as it sounds).

CHAPTER TEN
It's A Marathon, Not a Sprint

—

Setting your standards is important. Maintaining your standards is *importanter*.

I don't subscribe to the idea of the "honeymoon phase" of a relationship. I think the entire relationship should be a honeymoon phase.

THAT'S RIGHT, I SAID IT.

And I don't care if you think it's unrealistic.

I believe that the healthiest relationships last over time because both teammates put in consistent effort to show the other how much they mean and what they bring to the partnership. Not once a week, not once a month — but constantly. Romance and affection should not fade over time — in fact — I believe when a partnership is right, you'll experience just the opposite.

My personal opinion is that as your relationship continues to evolve, your partner becomes a larger, more important part of your life. Why would this mean you should be *less* romantic with them? Because you've already "gotten them"? No, actually, on the contrary.

As the man or woman in your life becomes more integrated and more "one" with you, you learn more about them. As you learn more about them, you learn the small nuances that make them feel special. Their little preferences, their routines, their favorite brand of coffee, the fact that they rescued a turtle once and now it's a fun anecdote you both refer back to. Small things — that really are big things. This means you have *infinitely* more opportunities to make this person feel special, because you know things about them that other people don't know.

You are both evolving, changing human beings, and that means your relationship never has to get old.

But, James, it's the same person for the rest of your life!

Oh, is it? I ask you, are you the same person you were ten years ago? Five years ago? One year ago? I know I'm not. I have learned, and grown, and evolved, and failed, and overcome challenges, and changed my perspective on life due to new experiences. And, as I continue to progress, I will certainly not be the same person in another five years. Neither will you. Neither will the person you're dating, or married to.

I think this is why, when we hear about people staying

together for decades, it almost feels like a foreign concept to us. Almost as if you are suggesting someone — *gasp* — stay at the same job for their entire lives. What was once considered normal is now so outside of our realities, that we would go insane if we couldn't keep ourselves perpetually stimulated by jumping from startup to startup. Pension? What does that mean, Dad?

STOP LIGHTING FIREWORKS, START STOKING FIRES.

This long-term view of the world that previous generations held was based off of one value: *Commitment.* They were willing to work at something, to fix it when it needed fixing (unless it was just trashed, in which case, recognize it, drop that shit, and run). Their future selves would uphold the promises that their present selves had made — that is what commitment is all about.

Now, though, we light off fireworks. What I mean is we have this beautiful, bright, exciting display, and it looks amazing. Then, before you know it, it's over and all that's left is smoke and a blurred outline of what once existed.

Older generations would set fires. They would allow it to smolder, and stoke it accordingly as it would build up momentum. They would tend to it and take care of it and understand that if they wanted it to last, they were going to have to maintain it. Then, once it really began to take form, they would continue adding more wood to it, more stoking, more tending. They knew that if they left it alone for too long, it would eventually extinguish itself.

This, I believe, is what's missing in today's dating culture. The willingness to consistently tend to our fires and keep the flame burning. We expect to be able to walk out of the room, or leave it alone, and come back after an undetermined length of time to find the home fires burning just as strong as when we left. That's not how it works.

You get someone's attention by putting in effort. You *keep* someone's attention by putting in *more effort*. And you *continue* to show them you care by putting in even more effort.

I think we take commitment for granted. We figure that once someone is committed to us, that's it. We've got them now *insert evil laugh.* Sorry, you're going to have to try harder than that. Consistently.

Comfort in a relationship could be a good thing, and it could be a bad thing. The type of comfort with your significant other that allows you to open up to them, tell them your innermost secrets and desires, to be goofy with them, to use weird little baby or puppy voices with them — *that is a good kind of comfort.*

The bad type of comfort is that which leads to *complacency* in which one (or both) partners begin to feel taken for granted. This is where romance starts to fade. This is where the mystery disappears. This is where there is nothing left to the imagination. No more spark. No more fire. No more stoking the flame. We have to *build comfort over time*, just as we stoke the flame over time.

You don't need to perform grand romantic gestures every single day; these things can be a bit much (and get a little expensive). Your ability to be romantic is not tied to your bank balance — it is about how thoughtful and creative you're willing to be towards someone that you care about. How much attention are you willing to pay to *what makes them feel special?* Did you grab a pack of their favorite candy today at the convenience store? Did you get them a little stuffed animal that reminded you of something you've been talking about? Did you make sure you came back from the coffee shop with something for them, too?

You see, romance isn't something you do. It is not a purchase you make, or a date you go on, or a special anniversary celebration. Romance is so much more than that. Romance is something you embody in your very existence. It is something you exude from your pores when you so much as think of the person you love. It is something you feel. It is something you express.

Romance is something you are — and once you find the right person who brings it out in you, once you unlock this love within yourself — *it is something you will always be.*

It is something you will always be with the one person you choose to *commit* yourself to. Ah, that word again. Commitment. When we think of commitment in regard to today's relationships, we primarily think it means being with one person. Monogamy. Not cheating. You are committed to that person.

COMMIT TO COMMITMENT.

I think, though, it is a word that is thrown around too easily. Much like how we "love" people we barely know and "hate" people we have never met. Words that once had deep meaning and were reserved for those experiences of being gripped at your very core by the emotion you were expressing, have begun to lose their meaning due to overuse.

Using words like *love* in a brand new relationship where we have not experienced enough of a person to truly know them, waters down the term for those who actually mean it. For those who have built and created it alongside their partner for years. For those who value it for what it is —a deep, meaningful connection with another person that cannot be replaced.

When we say we love someone, we are expressing what I feel to be a commitment to that person. It is a pledge to stand by their side and be part of their life even when challenges arise. You do not walk away from someone you love. You do not constantly fight with someone you love. You do not lie to, or disrespect someone you love. This is what love means.

You commit to someone you love. You feel the pain they feel and you lend them your strength to overcome their challenges. You are the person they can count on to be left standing when all of the dust settles.

There is a famous quote by Orebela Gbenga which I think nicely outlines the idea of commitment: *"Commitment means staying loyal to what you said you were going to do long after the mood you said it in has left you."*

This translates easily to relationships – when you commit to someone, you are committing to all of them. You are committing to their positive qualities and their negative qualities. You are committing to be there during their sunny days and to hold the umbrella over you both during their rainy days.

You are committing to someone's whole self. You are not just committing to them under the condition that they stay young and beautiful – because they will not. And neither will you. You are not just committing to them until someone better comes along – you are committing to the idea that there is nobody better for you. You are committing to their very being. To them as a person. To the idea that the two of you are the consistent center and your circumstances simply orbit around you.

We are losing this idea of commitment. We are jumping into relationships too soon. We are making life-altering decisions alongside people we barely know. We are a society of convenience, instant gratification, and unstable loyalty. As we change phones for the newer advanced one, we are doing the same with relationships.

We are replacing each other as if memories were never shared. As if traditions were never built. As if we were not ever together as one, both emotionally and physically.

We symbolically erase each other by deleting old photos

off of Facebook and social media – effectively deleting someone's entire existence from our past. In doing so, we are deleting parts of ourselves. Memories. Experiences that made us who we are today. It has become so easy to just… forget, and move on.

Of course, people grow apart. Hurt, lies, and betrayal break up relationships. Nothing and nobody is perfect – and we cannot be expected to stay committed to someone who has broken our trust or their commitment to us. But aside from these circumstances, commitment is not a matter of convenience – it is a matter of one's word being their bond.

Commitment is not just an arbitrary word that can be found in the dictionary. It is not just a statement of temporary monogamy. It is a pledge, a vow, a way of living that embodies honor and integrity. Commitment is not a rule, or a regulation – it is an action.

Commitment is not the act of losing your freedom, but exercising it to choose who you want to give your most valuable gifts to: *Your time, your emotions, and your heart.*

Chapter Ten

Ah — here we are again. Placing enough value on yourself to be selective about who benefits from your presence in their life. I think that we are so caught up in trying to get people's attention (how am I supposed to compete with all of these Instagram models?!) that we forget to be discerning about who actually *deserves* it.

This chapter is about maintaining your standards over time — and frankly — it really holds true in all other areas of life, whether you are single or in a relationship, applying equally to your fitness routine, your job, your entrepreneurial endeavors, and marriage. The moment you begin to lower your expectations for the people around you, is the moment they begin to put in less effort towards you. Perhaps as one of the expectations you hold for your employees, they are required to fill out a daily or weekly form to keep you abreast on projects or developments — do you think they are going to continue filling out that form if you stop asking for it? Probably not.

Perhaps you've set a fitness goal for yourself, but instead of being in the gym five days a week, you have decided you'd like to sleep in a couple of times, and you're showing up thrice a week. Do you think you're going to progress at the same pace you were before? Probably not.

Perhaps you've decided that since you're now in a committed relationship, you can accept a bit more apathy from your partner, and put in less effort for them as well. I mean, you *are* committed to each other after all, right? When we apply this same thought process to our relationship, it's easy to see why we need to *keep dating* our partner. To *keep putting in effort.* To keep courting him or her.

BEING LOVED BY YOU IS A PRIVILEGE, NOT A RIGHT.

If it sounds like work, that's because it is. Being loved by someone is a privilege, but it's not a right. Privileges are earned, not gifted. I remember a long time ago reading an article online about how some high schools through the United States were going to stop keeping score at football games in order to avoid making the losing team feel too badly about themselves. There is also the *Mercy Rule* which prevents a team from winning by too many points – which, I guess I can understand. Sort of.

I played sports all of my life up until I reached college. Some I was better at than others. A little known fact is that I was a martial arts instructor also, teaching multiple forms of martial arts which I translated into varsity wrestling in high school. Whenever I would lose a match, I would watch the video in the following days, practice, and adjust. So did the rest of our team. I liked wrestling, because even though it is a team sport, it is also an individual sport.

We had two separate records: team and individual. This meant that while we were responsible for our own actions, we also had a vested interest in helping the rest of our teammates improve as well. Holding them to certain standards. Helping them along the way with strategies we had learned to be effective in our own matches. Not much else motivated people to get better though, besides losing.

You may be asking yourself by now, what does this have to do with dating and relationships? Well, quite a bit, actually.

You see, as men and women, we are responsible for our individual lives – just like my teammates and I were, on the wrestling team. But we are also all progressing forward as one in some ways. The way we act towards each other is the perception that we carry into our next interaction with others. It may not be fair, it may start us behind the 8-ball when we have done nothing wrong, but it is reality. And it makes us all responsible, because we are all connected in that way.

We can still win as individuals. You can be the best wrestler on the team and win all of the individual titles, but only if you put in your own individual work and effort to rise above the rest of your teammates. You cannot coast along and just accept your trophy because other people on the team are good. This goes for life as well.

And this is what is happening lately. We are giving trophies just for showing up. We are afraid to criticize others because we might hurt their feelings. We are afraid to make anything exclusive because some people will feel left out. We have stopped keeping score in the game of life.

What this leads to is something called entitlement. Men are feeling entitled to women's bodies, women are feeling entitled to men's money. Men feel they have the right to a woman because they took her on a date or paid her a compliment or did something nice for her. Women are feeling entitled to free dinners and drinks because they've been conditioned to expect it. And when something doesn't work out, they are both reacting to rejection in a "how dare you reject me" manner and it is making everyone look bad.

This is not how any of this works.

In my opinion, being in an exclusive relationship with someone is one of the highest compliments they can give you. Here is a person who has the opportunity to choose one person out of seven billion in the world to intimately commit themselves to. When they choose you, it is a privilege that should be taken seriously.

Nobody is entitled to anyone else. Nobody owes anything to anyone. Acts of kindness for the sake of a reward are not truly kindness – they are bribes. We have to start valuing each other as human beings and letting go of the idea that we have the right to be in a relationship.

We don't.

The harsh reality is that you do not inherently deserve anyone's love just because you are you. And they do not deserve your love, just because they are them. If they have not put in the proper effort to become the right kind of person, and also to show you how much you mean to them, in order to build an emotional bond with you – then they have not earned the opportunity to be with you. It is that simple.

You are not a participation trophy. You are not something that someone gets just because they happened to show up first. Plus, nobody puts a participation trophy on their mantel. There is pride in earning something that not everybody gets. Something that requires effort to be part of, and then effort to stay connected with. A relationship with you is this something.

You are a championship trophy, reserved only for the one

who puts the work and effort into becoming the person who truly deserves you – and it's time somebody told you that.

More than that, though, it's time somebody *didn't have to* tell you that. It's time that you understand you are worthy of love. It's time that you understand you should be valued, adored, cared for, and supported. It's time that you understand your intrinsic value, and that you stop devaluing yourself for people who don't deserve you. Men and women alike get taken advantage of, rejected, discouraged, and begin to question their self-worth because society too often ingrains in us that we must compromise our happiness in order to maintain a surface connection with someone else.

Stop letting the world dictate your value. Stop letting the opinions of others change how you see yourself. Stop thinking that someone's inability to see your worth makes you less worthy of love. *It does not.* You are a kind, genuine, caring person, who is willing to give love to others. In a world where we witness violence and betrayal and dishonesty every single day, these qualities make you almost *superhuman*.

You are *not* reading this book because you are like everyone else. This book is not for everyone. This book is for the people who want to *create love within themselves, and then share it with the world.* This book is for the people who are conscious. Who are awake. Who are striving to live their best life and to make a positive impact on society. This book is for people who smile at strangers. This book is for people who listen to others and provide advice. This book is for people who open up their hearts to those they care about — and even to those they don't know.

I know this is you. I know this is you because I've spoken to you. I've heard from you. I've listened. I've observed. I've read your comments, and your messages. I have seen your frustrations. I have felt your pain.

I know this is you because I have experienced the rejection, I have worked through the heartache, I have wondered where I went wrong. I have questioned *my own* value. I have allowed others to make me feel inadequate and unworthy of love or respect. And, I know this is you because you've read this book. People who do not seek to create love would not be be spending their precious time reading these words right now.

I know this is you because no matter what race, gender, sexual orientation, nationality, or age that you are — we are one. We are beings of love, and we are all bound together through this reality. I believe that each of us wants to be loved, cared for, and adored, regardless of any other life circumstances. I believe that we are all searching for happiness, and that we all have the ability to create it within ourselves, regardless of our relationship status.

Imagine, if we could all internalize this truth and realize that love and the search for happiness is what brings us all together. Imagine if we could fully realize that we all feel the same emotions, that we all seek pleasure and avoid pain. Imagine if we all filled ourselves up with self-love to the point where we had no choice but to allow it to overflow onto the people around us.

Imagine if we approached every single person we meet with the understanding that they are going about their day in the best way they know how. Imagine if we could help *even one person* to find this love and happiness within themselves. Imagine if you could take someone on this journey and help them *unlock the love they desire and deserve.*

WHAT A WORLD IT WOULD BE.

—

A SPECIAL THANK YOU

—

Before I acknowledge some of the special people in my life, and in the creation of this book, I want to take a second to thank someone who may not get the recognition they always deserve:

YOU.

That's right, as a writer, speaker, and now — author — I fully understand the fact that without *you*, none of this would be possibly. This book would simply have remained a dream, and my blog simply would have blended in with the hundreds of millions of others floating around on the internet. It would not have been read over 37 million times, we would not have a community of over 300,000 people on social media, and you would definitely not have this book in your hands right now.

You may notice that I speak as "we," and not "I." That is because I understand that everything in life is a team effort. Regardless of what kind of relationship we may be talking about, whether it is intimate, personal, professional, or otherwise, it requires at least two people in order to make it work. In my relationship with you, my words would fall on deaf ears if it were not for you reading them, sharing them, absorbing them, and living them. My life experiences would simply stop inside my own mind and not be able to help someone else who may need it.

I cannot reach millions of people by myself. I am not a famous celebrity who can send a single tweet and change the course of a fashion trend or expose an entire country to a new artist or superstar. I am but one man from a suburban town outside of Boston who has chosen to document his experiences in life along the way.

Fortunately for me (and those who have been helped by my writing), *you* have taken hold of my experiences, thoughts, viewpoints, and opinions, and shared them with the world. It is only your dedication and consistency that keeps me in a position to keep talking about these subjects in a manner and through a forum that allows others to listen. A lack of an audience does not inspire the growth of one.

So, I use this as an opportunity to express my gratitude to you. I thank you for being willing to absorb these concepts, I thank you for expressing love and compassion to the world. I thank you for being proof that the want (and need) for love, romance, respect, and chivalry, is still very much alive and well when others think it has faded into obsolescence.

I thank you for joining me on my journey, and taking me with you on yours. Carry this book with you as a reminder that no matter where you are in your life or in the world, you will always have love, because it is within you.

ACKNOWLEDGEMENTS

—

There is no way to thank all of the people who have come into my life over the past few decades, and made a positive impact on it. If you do not see your name here, please do not underestimate the role that you have played in bringing me to this point. If I have ever had a single conversation or interaction with you, I have learned something from you that has helped mold me into the person I am today.

My parents, Jim and Lisa.

I would be nowhere without my parents. They have been my friends, my confidants, my inspiration, my support system, my safety net, my sounding board, my shelter, and my cheerleaders, for 32 years. There are no words that can be written to express what they have brought to my life. My parents taught me what it means to be a good man.

My brother, Blake.

My brother will forever be my best friend and one of the most kindhearted, genuine people that I know. I learn from him every day simply by observing the way he lives his life. To be as successful, multi-talented, driven, and ambitious as him will forever be a goal of mine. He has supported me and helped me out of a bind on more than a few occasions. I would not be the man I am today if I had anyone else as a brother.

My grandparents, Silvio and Elena.

While I didn't always agree with my grandfather, he taught me an endless amount of lessons about life, and love. He was rooted deeply in the old school, and he helped me understand what unconditional love is. He always believed I was going to do great things. He is part of the reason I finally moved to Los Angeles. He would tell Blake and me to "walk straight, and fly right." He'd tell me to "kick it in the ass." He would read all of my articles and talk to me about his ideas. He loved my grandmother for more than 64 years before drawing his last breath in December of 2016. My grandmother — who, to this day, wears his jewelry on special occasions. She tells me he would be proud of what I'm doing, and that she is, too. She has always been the peacekeeper and the one who would try to bind family together — for better or worse — but she showed me what it means to always have your heart at the root of compassion.

Jaime and Bobby.

My sister and her husband, who I don't see often enough (that's what happens when you guys live in Hawaii!), but who exemplify the fun and freshness that can stay in a relationship over the long term. Like two kids in a candy store, they have helped to show me that love and romance doesn't have to be so serious. Have fun with each other, act like children, keep the youth alive.

Dave Humphrey.

Dave has been a longtime friend of mine who has been one of those rare people outside of your family that you can always count on. He exemplifies what it means to be a man who lives his life selflessly, whether it is towards his wife, his six children, or a stranger on the street.

Alexandra Adomaitis.

A muse, if there ever was one. Alexandra helped me to finally take the leap into writing this book after I saw the success she had with her own book, *The Art of Being a Woman*. She is an inspiration to all who know her, and living proof that class still exists in the world.

Rick Schirmer and Rachel McCord.

My fantastic new Hollywood friends who introduced me to my video producer and web designer, Brandon.

Brandon Rogers.

Without your video and web-design skills, we wouldn't have such an awesome ecosystem in which this book was able to come to fruition. Appreciate all of your work, brother!

Emily Covi.

The phenomenal designer of the cover of this book, who worked super quickly and efficiently to get a beautiful final copy finished on short notice. View more of her work at FueledDesigns.com

Leeann Gudzinowicz.

Leeann is one of the best photographers I have ever worked with; the photo on the back cover of this book is credited to her, along with many others. Cannot possibly recommend this woman more.

Jerri Newman.

Jerri is an old friend of my parents, and a kindhearted soul willing to bring years of experience to a new author (me) in the form of editing this book to its full potential. I have Jerri to thank for being my second set of eyes and for helping to refine the tone and structure of my writing to get my points across as effectively and articulately as possible.

Katy Newman.

A testament to staying in touch with people through the years, Katy grew up in the same town as I did (shout out to Arlington, Massachusetts), and noticed on Facebook that I'd been writing this book. She suggested I contact her mother about editing— not that I ever make any typos! Katy not only brought Jerri in to edit the book, but Katy herself can be credited with the final round of edits and all of the beautiful formatting you see across these pages. Without Katy, this wouldn't have been such a clean reading experience for you.